Beautiful City

Beautiful City
The Dialectical Character
of Plato's "Republic"

DAVID ROOCHNIK

Cornell University Press

Ithaca and London

First published 2003 by Cornell University Press

Printed in the United States of America

Library of Congress Cataloging-in-Publication Data

Roochnik, David.
    Beautiful city : the dialectical character of Plato's "Republic" /
David Roochnik.
        p. cm.
Includes bibliographical references and index.
    ISBN 0-8014-4087-4 (alk. paper)
    1. Plato. Republic. I. Title.
    JC71 .R66 2003
    321'.07—dc21

                                                    2002151028

 Cornell University Press strives to use environmentally
responsible suppliers and materials to the fullest extent possible in the publishing of its books. Such materials include veg-
etable-based, low-VOC inks and acid-free papers that are
recycled, totally chlorine-free, or partly composed of
nonwood fibers. For further information, visit our website at
www.cornellpress.cornell.edu.

Cloth printing   10 9 8 7 6 5 4 3 2 1

This book is dedicated,
with love and gratitude,
to my daughters,
Lena and Shana

Contents

ACKNOWLEDGMENTS   ix

PROLOGUE   1

CHAPTER ONE. The Arithmetical
  1. Tripartite City, Tripartite Soul   10
  2. The One, the Two, and the Three   30
  3. The Arithmetical Character of Kallipolis   40

CHAPTER TWO. Eros
  1. Intimations of Eros   51
  2. The Three Waves   57
  3. Kallipolis v. the *Republic*   69

CHAPTER THREE. Democracy, Psychology, Poetry
  1. Democracy   78
  2. Narrative Psychology   93
  3. Psychological Narrative   111

APPENDIX. The Meaning of "Dialectical"
  1. The Technical Meaning of "Dialectic"   133
  2. The Nontechnical Meaning of "Dialectic"   140
  3. Dialectic in the *Republic*   149

BIBLIOGRAPHY   153

INDEX   157

Acknowledgments

I am grateful to my teacher, Stanley Rosen. His essay "The Role of Eros in Plato's *Republic*," which he originally delivered as a lecture in 1964, was one inspiration for this book. Another was a conversation I had with Dan O'Connor when I was a visiting professor at Williams College in 1992. Dan, who had heard about the rather odd way I was teaching the *Republic*, came into my office and asked me to explain it to him. It's taken me ten years.

My friends Alessandra Fussi and Alfredo Ferrarin have helped me to think about Plato, and they have been remarkably encouraging in a variety of ways. So too have my colleagues Brian Jorgensen, Allen Speight, Stephanie Nelson, and Greg Fried. They heard me lecture on the *Republic* more than once, and I'm grateful for what they had to say in response. Jay Samons read the whole manuscript, made many comments, and has become a valuable and provocative interlocutor. The students in the various Plato seminars I have taught for the past few years at Boston University have been a pleasure to work with and a consistent source of energy. Charles Griswold, the chairman of my department and an old friend, has always been supportive. Drew Hyland, both teacher and friend, has influenced me from the beginning.

None of the work reflected in this book would have been worthwhile to me if I hadn't always been able to return home to my family. My wife, Gina Crandell, and my daughters, Lena and Shana, are where my days begin and end.

D.R.

Beautiful City

Prologue

In this short book I explain and describe in detail the philosophical character of Plato's *Republic*. It is, I argue, a thoroughly dialectical work.

For many years I believed that the notion of a short book on Plato's masterpiece was absurd. What is finally most impressive about the *Republic* is its extraordinary level of internal coherence. Whereas smaller dialogues, such as the *Laches*, *Charmides*, and *Apology*, are like beautiful jewels whose dazzling structure can be apprehended because of the limited magnitude of the whole, the *Republic* achieves the same level of tight unity but on a vast scale. As a result, in the past I found it impossible to comment in a satisfying way on any single part of the *Republic*—say the divided-line passage of book 6—without factoring in, and then losing myself in, the surrounding whole in which it is embedded. This was a sobering, even frustrating experience, and it caused me to write little on the work that I believe is the most philosophically rich of them all.

I have often wondered whether the only honest response to the *Republic* would be a comprehensive, line-by-line commentary. The challenge posed by such a task is more than daunting, however, and for just the reason stated above: since the *Republic* exhibits a powerfully coherent structure, commenting on each of its parts would require continually invoking the principles by means of which they cohere. By necessity, then, such a commentary would become far longer than the dialogue itself, for it would include an exegesis of each part, as well as a continually reiterated and expanded explanation of how it contributes to and is integrated into the whole.

Ultimately, perhaps, this burden is a legitimate one to place upon the serious commentator. Living as I do in an impatient time, however, I have chosen not to pursue this line of work. Instead, I have focused on a limited theme that I describe as the "character" of the *Re-*

public. I articulate and defend a conception of what sort of philosophical work the *Republic* is. And I am calling it dialectical.

Such a theme might seem to be merely stylistic, but what is at stake is not merely a question of style. Uncovering and articulating the dialectical character of Plato's work provides a unique form of access to its many parts. To cite a salient example: despite appearances to the contrary, especially passages from book 8, the *Republic* actually offers a qualified and cautious defense, rather than a resounding condemnation, of democracy. This defense, however, is specifically dialectical. In other words, it is not stated as an isolated political thesis expounded explicitly and then substantiated at a particular juncture of the work. Instead, it emerges from the dialogue as a whole, from the very fabric of the work understood as a dialectical activity which, as Socrates says, is "probably" possible only in a democracy (see *Republic* 557d).

I make a similar argument concerning the issue of what today is called "diversity": that is, the affirmation of the goodness and political value of a multiplicity of human types, beliefs, characters, attitudes, and so on. No dialogue could seem to be more hostile to this view than the *Republic*, yet ultimately, the dialogue offers a defense of diversity. Once again, no independently standing bit of text can secure this thesis; it emerges only from an understanding of the dialogue—a work constituted by its many diverse parts—as a whole.

The key point here is that from an argument concerning the character or form of the *Republic*, specific and positive arguments about its content can be extracted. As the previous two paragraphs suggest, understanding Plato's dialogue as dialectical can lead to a further understanding of, among other things, his political views.

As to method: I begin with Plato's psychology, his *logos* of the *psychē*, and continually rely on it as a guiding thread. (Throughout this book I use, quite reluctantly, the word "soul" to translate the Greek *psychē*.)[1] I will show how the conception of the soul which Socrates articulates in his famous "tripartite psychology" in book 4 is both partial and provisional and how, commencing with the interruption that opens book 5, it is progressively revised. The subsequent sections of the dialogue, books 5–7 and then 8–10, each contains an increasingly more complex, richer, and more truthful psychology than

---

1. *Psychē* as "soul" has potentially dangerous implications. Often it is closer to "the nonmaterial aspect of a human being's life" than to what we typically conceive of as "soul."

what Socrates presents in book 4. Despite such revision, the book 4 account is not simply negated or junked as the *Republic* unfolds. Instead, it is preserved in its partiality as a moment of the dialectical development of the dialogue as a whole. My defense of this claim is detailed and, if successful, will stand as a paradigm by which the philosophical character of the *Republic* can best be appreciated.

The conception of dialectic that I hold should be slowly coming into view. In the appendix to this book I address the various technical meanings of "dialectic" as the word appears in the dialogues and as it has been discussed in the secondary literature. At this point, however, I clarify this term only by means of briefly discussing the most important single transition occurring in the *Republic*.

At the end of book 4, Socrates announces that he has completed his articulation of both a just regime and a just soul. As a result, at the beginning of book 5 he is poised to move on to the next stage of the dialogue: a discussion of the "four forms of badness" (449a) as they appear in both city and citizen. In other words, he is ready to address the four "mistaken" (544a) regimes and their corresponding soul types. He is, however, interrupted and sent on a long detour, one not ending until book 8. Polemarchus, joined by Adeimantus and then both Glaucon and Thrasymachus, "arrest" Socrates. They force him to return to a proposal he had made but had not adequately explained: "that, as for women and children, the things of friends will be in common" (449c). They are disturbed by the communalization of sexual relations and the replacement of the family by the city in the rearing of children. In their eyes, Socrates had treated this stunningly radical proposal with undue casualness, and so they demand that he return to it. Socrates consents but adds the following caveat:

> What a thing you've done in arresting me, I said. How much discussion [*logos*] you've set in motion, from the beginning again as it were, about the regime I was delighted to think had already been described, content if one were to leave it at accepting these things as they were stated then. You don't know how great a swarm of arguments you're stirring up with what you are now summoning to the bar. I saw it then and passed by so as not to cause a lot of trouble [*ochlon*]. (450a–b)

Socrates, it seems, would have been glad to be done with the just city at the end of book 4. But he is brought back to it by his young interlocutors' concern with sex. His methodical sequence of topics has been interrupted by Eros (whose primary meaning in Greek is "sexual desire"). As a result, the *logos* is "set in motion," for it must be revised and expanded. It must never be forgotten that what follows, the famous central portion (books 5–7) of the *Republic*, is explicitly a detour or digression sparked by this unexpected intrusion of Eros into the conversation.

Socrates professes to fear the "swarm" of arguments the interruption will unleash. They will, he suggests, cause "trouble." The Greek here is *ochlon* (450b2), which also means "crowd, throng, or mob." This is a word with antidemocratic connotations, for it has the specifically political sense of "populace or multitude."[2] He also says that the interruption will cause the *logos* to return to "the beginning [*ex archēs*: 450a8] again." Eros forces Socrates to return to the source, the origin, the heart of the discussion. The ensuing revisions, however unwieldy, must take place at a fundamental level.

In the chapters to follow I argue that the *Republic* has three distinct stages: books 2–4, books 5–7, and books 8–10. (Book 1, as Socrates himself describes it at 357a, is a "prelude.")[3] The first stage finds Socrates, aided by Glaucon and Adeimantus, constructing "in speech" a just city. This city has a tripartite class system, which in turn (because of the city-soul analogy at work) is instrumental in Socrates' development of a tripartite psychology. The interruption at the beginning of book 5 signals the inadequacy of this first stage. Something is missing, and it is Eros. The subsequent two stages supplement or remedy this deficiency. Each puts increasing emphasis on Eros and thereby moves the dialogue to a higher and more adequate level. That each negates the previous stage is especially striking in the increasingly sophisticated and expressive, the increasingly eroticized (and hence dangerous) psychology developed throughout the second and third stages of the dialogue.

Because they introduce philosophical issues of the highest order, books 5–7, as every reader recognizes, manifestly represent a great advance over the preceding material. Indeed many readers, spellbound by Socrates' three images of the sun, the line, and the cave, as well as

2. See *Symposium* 174a, where Socrates says he fears the "crowd."
3. I reject the arguments of Vlastos (1971) and others who believe that book 1 was written earlier. Throughout, my comments on book 1 cumulatively support the claim that it is an integral "prelude."

his discussion of mathematics in book 7, often identify these "metaphysical" and "epistemological" sections as the crux of the *Republic*. My interpretation places a great deal more emphasis on books 8–10 than is usual. I argue that the relationship between this third stage of the dialogue and the second must be conceived in the same sense as the second was in relation to the first: that is, as a dialectical negation or revision. Despite their extraordinary richness, even their seductiveness, books 5–7 contain but a partial view of the human soul, one in need of revision and supplementation. These arrive only in the third stage of the *Republic*.

To reformulate my thesis, I borrow Socrates' own metaphor of the three waves, which he uses in book 5 to describe the three conditions for the possibility of the just city: (1) "Men and women must share all pursuits in common" (457c). Most notably, women must be given the opportunity to rule the city. (2) "Women are to belong to all these men in common, and no woman is to live privately with any man. And the children, in their turn, will be common" (457d). This is the elimination of the family and the "communalization" or "politicalization" of all sexual relations. (3) Philosophers must "rule as kings" (473c).

The image of the three waves is apparently borrowed from nautical lore. Waves come in threes, each increasing in magnitude and severity. The third is thus the most difficult to swim through. The Greek is *kuma*, from the verb "to swell." It refers to any kind of "swelling," not just that of the sea, and specifically is used to name the "fetus," the swelling of the pregnant woman.

The *Republic*, conceived as a dialectical work, is a series of swellings. An early stage of the conversation is interrupted and then revised in an increasingly rich and more adequate manner. In a dialectical development an earlier stage is not, however, totally discarded as being simply wrong. Instead, even if partial or one-sided, it is nonetheless—though modified and thereby negated by the more complete accounts that follow it—preserved in its very partiality as a stage or moment of the entire development. A partial account can have real value, especially if its partiality is acknowledged as such. Once again, the concrete case used to illustrate this abstract conception is the psychology of book 4.

The sense of "dialectic" I have been describing makes use of Hegelian terminology, specifically the language of the *Aufhebung*. As Hegel puts it, *Aufheben* "has a twofold meaning in the language; on the one hand it means to preserve, to maintain, and equally it also means to cause to cease, to put an end to. Even 'to preserve' includes a negative element, namely, that something is removed from its immediacy and so from an existence which is open to external influences, in order to preserve it. Thus what is *Aufgehoben* is at the same time preserved; it has only lost its immediacy but is not on that account annihilated" (Hegel 1969, 107).

The word typically used to translate *Aufheben*, "sublate," is meaningless in ordinary English. But Hegel's notion is not. Hegelian dialectic conceives of various "moments" or stages of a rational development. An earlier stage of a dialectical exposition is negated by a later one. It is not, however, jettisoned. Its partiality is preserved as a stage or moment of the more comprehensive final account. The latter is richer, but a dimension of its richness is precisely its incorporation of the previous, partial moments. The familiar Hegelian way of expressing this point is to say that "the true is the whole" (Hegel 1977, 11).

In spite of its obvious debt to Hegel, my articulation of Platonic dialectic differs radically. (I include a more technical treatment of this issue, as well as secondary works that have commented on it, in the appendix.) For the purpose of this prologue, I simply return to the passage in book 5 discussed above in order to explain. When Polemarchus, Adeimantus, Glaucon, and Thrasymachus interrupt Socrates, they force him to revise the first stage of the *Republic*. In particular, the tripartite psychology of book 4 must be modified in order to generate a more adequate account of Eros. A *logos* is set in motion, one which (because it has been impregnated by Eros) "swells"; that is, it becomes richer and better able to do justice to the human soul. But the tripartite psychology is not simply discarded. Instead, it becomes a critical moment of the *Republic* conceived as a whole. As I explain in detail in chapter 1, because of its structural or logical (or "arithmetical") perspective on the soul, the tripartite psychology discloses a great deal about our ordinary experience of mental phenomena. (In an analogous fashion, so too does the tripartite division of the city into three classes.) Yet however valuable and informative this perspective may be, it is nonetheless decisively limited. The source of its limitation is its strict obedience to what some scholars have identified as Plato's statement of the principle of noncontradiction (436b) but what I term "the Principle of Non-Opposition." Later developments in the second and especially the third stage of the dialogue dialectically negate the tripartite scheme, move beyond its governing principle, and thereby present a more adequate, more truthful account of the human soul.

As a final introductory note, consider an approach to the *Republic* quite different from my own. In a well-known essay, David Sachs (1997) finds Plato guilty of the "fallacy of irrelevance." To refute Thrasymachus, Socrates is required to show that "vulgar justice"—that is, the nonperformance of "behavior commonly judged immoral or criminal" (10)—implies happiness. Socrates, however, proves only that "Platonic justice" (having a well-ordered, harmonious soul) implies happiness. There is, Sachs argues, no necessary connection between Platonic and vulgar justice; hence, Socrates' argument, even if successful, is irrelevant.

There are (at least) two strategies to use against Sachs. (1) Show that Platonic justice does entail ordinary morality. If the soul is constituted in such a fashion, then the agent necessarily would not commit immoral acts. (This is the strategy of Vlastos 1971.) (2) Grant the irrelevance but then integrate it into a comprehensive reading of the *Republic*. The justice that Socrates articulates in book 4 may carry no necessary relationship to ordinary morality, but the reason might be that the *subject of the dialogue has changed*. The *Republic* is a philosophical conversation between (primarily) Socrates and Glaucon. It is initiated by a concern for vulgar morality, but as it develops, the issue is no longer justice as conventionally understood (see 500d, 518d, and 619d). As the focus of the conversation, ordinary justice is gradually replaced by philosophy itself, which in its essence is extraordinary.

The preceding is certainly no argument, but it at least suggests a basic difference between a dialectical approach and that of Sachs and Vlastos. For them, the *Republic* is a massive (and static) set of premises that contribute to the construction of an argument, which in turn can be evaluated either positively (i.e., as consistent [Vlastos]) or negatively (Sachs); it is thus permissible for the commentator to choose his or her premises from anywhere in the set and to rearrange them at will in order to construct the best (or worst) argument possible. By contrast, I read the *Republic* as a living conversation, as a massive instance of *dialegesthai*.[4] As in many conversations, its topics change. Earlier proposals are reconsidered and revised. There is considerable interruption and sometimes improvement. Sachs's accusation of irrelevance is therefore itself irrelevant. It is unfair to mea-

4. In this important but limited sense, I take my bearings from Strauss 1978.

sure later developments in the dialogue by a standard established so early.

To state the obvious: whether my conception of the *Republic* and the argument I use to defend it have any merit cannot be determined by these introductory remarks but only by the textual analysis to follow.

Before beginning, a few words on procedure. I use Allan Bloom's 1968 translation. Even if it is wooden, this work is a masterpiece of literalness and consistency. For close textual exegesis from an English text, it cannot be improved on. There are, however, moments when Bloom's passion for consistency obscures the meaning of a phrase, so I occasionally depart from his text, always indicating that I am doing so. The Greek text I refer to is John Burnet's edition. Any translations from dialogues other than the *Republic* are my own and are also based on Burnet. (These, however, are extremely rare. The goal of this book is to offer an interpretation only of the *Republic*, and not, say, "the development of Plato's political theory.")[5]

In quoting from the *Republic*, I typically note only the Stephanus number and letter: for example, 450a. In quoting a specific word from the Greek, such as *ochlon*, above, I am more precise, in this case 450b2.

Because of their familiarity or etymological affinity with English derivatives, I have incorporated several phonetically spelled Greek words into my technical vocabulary. These include *logos*, *technē*, *arithmos*, and *muthos*.

Whenever I use the name "Socrates," I refer only to the character in Plato's dialogues. Nothing whatsoever is asserted about the historical figure.

The literature on the *Republic* is unmanageably vast and presents the grave risk to the commentator, of losing touch with the primary text. I therefore restrict my secondary sources chiefly to those written in English during the past forty years or so.

Finally, I frequently use Socrates' own word "Kallipolis" (527c2), or "beautiful city," to refer to the city he constructs in books 2–8. Al-

---

5. This is the title of Klosko 1986. Although space constraints do not allow me to defend it here, my interpretive principle is that in reading Plato, the basic hermeneutical unit is the single dialogue rather than the corpus.

though it plays an undeniably important role, Kallipolis is not the sole expression or culmination of Plato's political theory. Instead, it is a dialectical moment that emerges at a specific juncture during the unfolding of the dialogue. It comes into being in book 2 but falls apart and fades from view by book 8. It is crucial to my argument that the project of building Kallipolis is distinct from—indeed, is in tension with—the ten books of the *Republic* conceived as a whole.

CHAPTER ONE

The Arithmetical

I. TRIPARTITE CITY, TRIPARTITE SOUL

In book 2 of the *Republic*, Socrates makes a promise to Adeimantus: "First we'll investigate what justice is like in the cities. Then, we'll go on to consider it in individuals" (368e). Socrates can recommend this sequence because of his earlier assumption that the city and the individual are isomorphic. They are, he said, like two sets of the same letters, one of which is larger. Both city and individual, he assumes, are intelligible wholes composed of discrete, identifiable elements or units. Since it is much "easier" (368e) to see (or read) the larger set, Socrates begins by constructing a city in speech. Once it is completed, its internal structure, and thereby its justice and injustice, will become visible. Since the isomorphism is presumed to hold, the same structure and conception of justice can then be transferred to the individual. As Socrates puts it, this procedure will work because of the "likeness of the bigger in the visible structure [*idea*] of the littler" (369a3).[1]

This, of course, is the famous "analogy of city and soul" on which the entire project of the *Republic* seems to depend. It is crucial to note, however, that at the very moment he proposes the analogy, Socrates also calls it into question. He does so in two ways. (1) When describing how useful it will be for reading the smaller set of letters first to read them written large, he says, "I suppose it would be a godsend to be able to consider the littler ones after having read these first, if of course, they do happen to be the same" (368d). His "if" clause should force the reader to wonder whether the isomorphism holds or not. In fact, his "if" should raise the more basic question of whether either city or soul is actually composed of letterlike entities

---

1. Klein (1977, 3) offers "look" as a translation. Bloom uses the English "idea" in this passage. Even though it exactly reproduces the Greek word, this translation obscures the fact that *idea* is not used here in the technical or metaphysical sense of a "Platonic idea." It also hides the etymological root of *idea* in the verb "to see."

to begin with. (2) Socrates twice mentions that treating the city as the individual written large will make his task "easier" (368e8, 369a9), a word Adeimantus himself eagerly repeats (370a6). Recall exactly what this task is. Because of what he says is his sense of piety (368b8), Socrates feels obligated to defend justice after it has been slandered so badly by Thrasymachus in book 1. The sophist has claimed, among other things, that "injustice is more profitable" to a man than justice (348b). Even though Socrates apparently refuted this assertion in book 1, both Glaucon and Adeimantus rejuvenate and amplify Thrasymachus's position at the beginning of book 2 in order to force Socrates to do a better job of defeating it.

In short, Socrates is engaged in a specific practical or dialogical situation at the outset of book 2. He must come to the aid of two young men who are not completely convinced of the desirability of leading a just life. He openly admits to taking an "easier" path: that is, treating city and soul as two isomorphically structured wholes, each of which is composed of discrete, letterlike elements, in order to accomplish his task.

When Socrates announces that the city he has been constructing in Books 2–4—to which he will later give the name "Kallipolis" ("beautiful city": 527c2)—has been successfully "founded" (427c6), he is ready to make good on his promises. He investigates political justice and arrives at the following definition: justice is "the practice of minding one's own business [*to ta hautou prattein*]" 433a8). A more literal translation of this phrase would be, "doing the things that belong to oneself": that is, performing one's proper activities and functions. By "one" here Socrates refers to each of the three distinct classes present in Kallipolis, which had earlier (415a) been symbolized by three metals: bronze, silver, and gold.[2] Justice, then, finds "the money-making [bronze], auxiliary [silver], and guardian [gold] classes doing what's appropriate, each of them minding its own business in a city" (434c). If the guardians rule and give orders, if the workers or moneymakers receive and obey orders, and if the auxiliaries help the rulers, then the city is without faction or discord and thus, given the definition, is just. To state it generally, and without going into any further detail here, justice is a kind of harmony (443d), the internal coherence or health (444d) of a smoothly functioning tripartite city.

2. I collapse the bronze and iron.

After completing this segment of the argument, Socrates is poised to make the all-important transition to the individual. Before doing so, he reiterates his guiding principles. (Note that Socrates repeats both of his earlier qualifiers, the "easy" and the "if.")

> If we should attempt to see justice first in some bigger thing that possesses it, we would more easily catch sight of what it's like in one man. And it was our opinion that this bigger thing is a city; so we founded one as best we could, knowing full well that justice would be in a good one at least. Let's apply what came to light there to a single man, and if the two are in agreement, everything is fine. (434d–e)

Shortly after this passage, Socrates significantly changes his terminology. He shifts from speaking of the "individual" or the "single man," as he had at 368e, to speaking of the "soul" (435c5). At this point, the body seems to drop out of the discussion. In any case, just as he had articulated the justice of the city on the basis of its internal structural coherence, so too must he articulate the structure of the soul. This Socrates can easily do: after all, the entire discussion has presupposed, even if in a qualified manner, the isomorphism of city and soul. Both are being treated like syllables or words: similarly shaped wholes composed of discrete, identifiable, letterlike elements or units. This is precisely what Socrates refers to when he says, "Isn't it quite necessary for us to agree that the very same forms and dispositions [*eidē te kai ēthē*] as are in the city are in each of us?" (435e). The key word is "forms," which, like *idea* at 369a3, does not carry a technical or metaphysical meaning in this sentence. Instead, it refers to a visible or intelligible shape or element, what Jacob Klein translates as a "look" (1977, 3). Since the city is essentially tripartite—containing as it does the three distinct "classes of natures" (435b5)—so too must the individual be. Corresponding to the three political divisions, then, are three "forms" (435c1) or identifiable elements of the soul: calculation (*logistikon*: 439d5), spirit (*to thumoeides*: 441a2), and desire (*epithumētikon*: 439d8).

(I consistently follow Bloom in translating *logistikon* as "calculation," rather than the more familiar "reason." The verb from which this noun derives means "to count, to calculate, to reckon, to compute." There is no mistaking its arithmetical overtones and these, as this chapter demonstrates, are central to Plato's strategy at this stage of the *Republic*.)

Here, then, is the initial articulation of what many scholars have designated as "the doctrine that the soul is tripartite, or that in each man's soul there are three 'parts,'" and which they further character-ize as a "standing feature of Plato's thought" (Crombie 1969, 341). Its most striking element is the sharp distinction Socrates draws be-tween calculation and desire. Many chronologically minded com-mentators believe that this is Plato's attempt to correct his earlier (or Socratic) denial of *akrasia*, or weakness of the will. Penner puts it thus: "The parts-of-the-soul doctrine is intended as a refutation of Socrates' view of *akrasia*" (1990, 96). If calculation and desire are two separate powers, it becomes possible to explain what seems to be an undeniable human experience: namely, knowing what is right but not doing it. This separation allows for the possibility of being over-powered by desire, a possibility seemingly denied in, for example, the *Protagoras* (see 352d–357).[3]

To justify this separation, Socrates offers the following argument, which begins with a general premise: "It's plain," he says, "that the same thing won't be willing at the same time to do or suffer opposites with respect to the same part and in relation to the same thing" (436b). The exact meaning of this passage is contested.[4] Is it, as some believe, the "the earliest explicit statement in Greek literature of the maxim of Contradiction" (Adam 1902, 246)? Julia Annas thinks not, because that "concerns propositions and their logical relations, whereas Plato is here concerned whether a certain thing can have cer-tain properties. Furthermore, he is concerned with opposites in a very broad sense, not just contradictories." As a result, she labels the statement "the principle of conflict" (Annas 1982, 137). Granting her basic point but preferring a negative in the formulation, I opt for the "Principle of Non-Opposition" (PNO).[5]

The PNO dominates the subsequent argument. Its next premise,

3. On this reading, the psychology of book 4 also improves upon Plato's "earlier" at-tempt in the *Phaedo* to explain this phenomenon by means of the conflict between soul and body. "Now [in the *Republic*] desires and emotions are attributed to the soul itself rather than to the body, and the soul has parts" (Miller 1999, 90). In general, as Gill (1985, 6) puts it, "In admitting the existence of non-rational elements in the *psuchē*, Plato is turning his back on the Socratic theory."

4. Bloom translates *kata tauton* (436b8) as "with respect to the same part." He fre-quently imports the word "part" when it does not appear in the Greek. Robinson (1971) and Stalley (1975) specifically take up this issue.

5. Miller (1999, 92) uses this same phrase. I arrived at it independently. The Kneales (1984, 11) claim that this is the Principle of Non-Contradiction. See *Sophist* 230b for a similar statement.

for example, specifies the sorts of opposites Socrates has in mind: "acceptance to refusal, longing to take something to rejecting it, embracing to thrusting away" (437b). What Socrates is most concerned to explain is the psychological phenomenon of seeming to experience both opposites simultaneously. His example is thirst, the desire for drink. (As I suggest below, Socrates' example, the desire for something wet, is subtly ironic: it is being used in the service of constructing a soul that is entirely dry.) It seems possible both to long to drink and also refuse to drink. But since these are opposite psychological experiences, they cannot emerge from the same form of the soul without violating the PNO. Therefore, "if ever something draws [the soul] back when it's thirsting, wouldn't that be something different in it from that which thirsts and leads it like a beast to drink?" (439b). Because the PNO is operative, a "second something" must draw the soul back when it refuses to drink. This something is calculation. The argument is complete, and so Socrates states his conclusion: "Let these two forms in the soul be distinguished" (439e).

To arrive at the third form, Socrates does not deploy an argument. Instead, and quite strangely, he tells a story: "I once heard something that I trust," he says (439e). He then recounts the story of Leontius, who, going up from the Piraeus, saw some corpses. He wanted to look, struggled not to (presumably because he thought it wrong to look), but finally was overcome by his desire. Yet after looking, he castigated his own eyes. "Look, you damned wretches, take your fill of the fair sight" (440a), he screamed at them. This capacity for righteous indignation, for anger, for competitive zeal, is spirit.[6] In the well-functioning soul the three forms work harmoniously. Each does its own job, which becomes the very definition of justice. Calculation rules, desire obeys, and spirit functions as the ally of calculation. Justice, in both city and soul, is construed as internal coherence, the absence of faction.

In outline, then, the above sketches both the tripartite psychology of book 4 and some of the background assumptions governing it. Commentators have been quick to go on the attack. Particularly targeted is the sharp distinction Socrates draws between calculation and desire. Annas succinctly states this objection: "Unfortunately . . .

6. Some scholars think that Socrates' story here makes fun of a known necrophiliac. More important by far is the way in which it prefigures later developments, specifically Socrates' increased use of narratives in books 8 and 9. This point is developed at length in chapter 3.

Plato has divided the soul into a totally irrational, craving part, and a rational, cognitive part. . . . The argument here gives us a wrong conception of desire" (1982, 139). A complementary objection would quickly follow, that because the book 4 conception of calculation is empty of desire, it is utterly ineffectual. The tripartite soul of book 4, on this highly critical view, is artificially compartmentalized, and the result is decidedly implausible. Human beings do not have within them either a totally irrational part or a part entirely bereft of desire.

On the basis of such a view, Bernard Williams (1997) has offered a sustained and compelling criticism of both the psychology of book 4 and the larger project in which it is embedded. He claims to uncover a deep "contradiction" implicit in the city-soul analogy. The city, he first says (drawing on 435e), obeys the "whole-part rule": "A city is F if and only if its men are F." In other words, a city is spirited if and only if its citizens are spirited. In turn, a city is (presumably) just if and only if its citizens are just. Recall, however, that for a man to be just, each of his three psychological elements must do its own job—implying, Williams says, that "logistikon [calculation] rules" (1997, 51). Applied to the city, this means that in a just city the "epithymetic" citizens who correspond to desire in the soul will be large in number and must be ruled by a small number of rational men. The problem, however, is that "an epithymetic man—surely—is not a dikaios [just] man" (52). Therefore, in a just city, most citizens are unjust, and the whole-part rule is violated.

To avoid this result, one might argue that each of the three classes of the city contains some measure of calculation, which rules them. On this view, "calculation . . . will be at work in each member even of the lowest and epithymetic class" (Williams 1997, 52). This is an attractive possibility because it would allow individual citizens to achieve the harmony of their three parts: that is, to be just. For Williams, however, this position, even if plausible when applied to the city, leads to absurdity when transferred back to the soul: "We shall reach the absurd result that epithumetikon in a just soul harkens to the logistikon in that soul through itself having an extra little logistikion of its own" (52). But what exactly is "absurd" about this? A diagram (figure 1) in which C stands for calculation, S for spirit, and D for desire should help.

In order to obey the dictates of calculation, a working-class citizen must have "an extra little" bit of calculation of his or her own. Hence, on the left side of the diagram, each class of citizens is shown

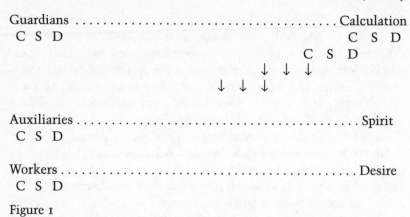

Figure 1

as having calculation, spirit, and desire. This makes sense; after all, a worker is a human being with a soul and therefore, since the soul is tripartite, should have each of the three parts. The problem comes when the isomorphism between city and soul is strictly held to and transferred to the right side of the diagram. Now each part of the soul has three parts within it. And each of the three parts has three parts. In short, the absurdity Williams claims to uncover is like a version of the homunculus problem. Explaining how the soul works, places entire souls within the soul. Each part of the soul becomes an entire person.[7] This is "absurd" because, as shown on the right of the diagram, it generates an indefinite expansion of the soul, which, on this view, is sparked into continual self-motion; that is, the number of its parts continually increases.

Williams accuses Plato of trying to "have it both ways" (1997, 53). He could conceive of the political correlate of desire: that is, the workers, as having within them some measure, however diminished, of calculation. If so, the problem outlined above occurs. On the other

7. Commentators such as Annas are alert to Williams's objection and attempt to ward it off. She appeals to a "top-down" brand of psychological theory in which the explanatory parts of the soul— calculation, spirit, and desire—do indeed share features of the whole soul, albeit in a far simpler way. Of these various parts she says, "It is easy to think of such an explanatory entity as being itself a homunculus. . . . But this is not necessarily objectionable, as long as one is clear that the item in question is meant to be something that is both simpler than the whole person with all their other functions and also something that shares features with the whole person. . . . Plato's parts of the soul are, I think, best thought of as just such a committee of relatively ignorant and narrow-minded homunculi" (Annas 1982, 144). See also Moline's discussion of "agents" (1978, 18).

hand, he could conceive of each of the three classes of the city as being strictly analogous to the part of soul to which that class corresponds. The rulers would be "totally logistic," the militaristic auxiliaries purely spirited, and the working class bereft of intelligence. On this picture, "a totally logistic ruling class [is] holding down with the help of a totally thymoeidic military class, a weakened and repressed epithymetic class" (53).

Williams is right to characterize this picture as "less attractive" (53). It is not only politically repulsive—that is, thoroughly repressive, transforming the majority of citizens into irrational nonhumans—but also psychologically inaccurate. The members of the working class are in fact human beings, and so they too must have souls. To restate the "ineliminable tension in Plato's use of his analogy" (54): Plato can restore humanity to the working class by reinjecting its members with a small bit of calculation, but when this move is translated back to the soul, the absurdity commences. To put the point more generally yet: to be human in any recognizable sense is to be rational. The tripartite psychology, however, postulates a totally irrational and hence seemingly inhuman part of the soul—namely, desire. A just soul is one in which the calculating part rules the desiring part. But without any calculation at all, how could such a part receive, understand, and obey orders? This problem, as Williams has shown, infects both the political and the psychological elements of the analogy.

A second set of commentators approach the tripartite psychology somewhat differently. Instead of seeing calculation and desire as radically distinct, Christopher Bobonich, for example, argues that the three parts of the soul "are themselves agent-like"; each part has its own desires, and each part "can engage in some form of calculating" (1994, 3–4). Glenn Lesses (1987, 149) makes the same point: "Appetite can engage in at least limited means-end practical calculating." He continues, "Each part of the soul," not just calculation, "is associated with beliefs." Charles Kahn agrees: "All three parts of the soul have a cognitive aspect and all three are also forms of desire" (1987, 91). Indeed, for Kahn, "the Platonic conception of calculation is a form of desire" (80). Calculation, he argues, "is . . . essentially desire for the good" (84).

To argue their point, these commentators rely on evidence from later books of the *Republic*. The first passage Bobonich (1994) cites, for example, is 580d3–587e4. Here (in book 9) Socrates reconceives and reformulates the three previously named psychological "forms"— calculation, desire, and spirit—as "wisdom-loving, victory-loving, gain-loving" (581c3). The repetition of the prefix *philo*-obviously signals what the putatively different forms share. Their commonality is affirmed in the next remarks Socrates makes: he assigns three pleasures to each of the three forms (581c6). If pleasure is conceived as the object of desire, this move suggests, as Terence Irwin puts it, that "the division of the soul is a division of desires" (1977, 328). A similarly unifying move occurs during the description of the money-loving part at 580e. Far from being an "irrational, craving part," it is now, to quote Annas, "capable of beliefs about how to attain fairly complex and long-range desires" (1982, 139).

In a similar fashion, John Cooper (1984) cites book 6, where the idea of the good is described as "that which every soul pursues." In addition, he observes that the democratic man described in book 8, whose life is ruled by the free expression of his various desires, does "a little philosophy." This, Cooper argues, shows that desire need not be restricted to the "basic recurrent biological urges" (1984, 9). Finally, on the basis of what Socrates says about spirit in books 8 and 9, he concludes that spirit is best understood as "the desire for esteem" (16).

These commentators do not justify, explain, or even bother to wonder why it is legitimate to refer to later books of the *Republic* in order to bolster the psychology of book 4. In other words, they fail to ask what sort of book it is whose later stages contain material that supplements or improves upon earlier ones. They do not ask why book 4 is inadequate in and of itself. Instead, they seem to treat the dialogue as a static whole, any of whose several parts can be extracted as independent propositions and then rearranged to supply premises for an argument.

Despite the glaring omission of necessary questions, in one important sense these commentators are quite right. That Plato does not ultimately conceive of calculation and desire as radically separate is indeed evidenced by later developments, especially in book 9. In fact, Socrates alludes to just this possibility even in book 4 when, precisely at the moment he begins sketching the tripartite psychology, he calls it into question:

Do we act in each of these ways a result of the same part of ourselves, or are there three parts and with a different one we act in
each of the different ways? Do we learn with one, become spirited
with another of the parts within us, and desire the pleasures of
nourishment and generation with a third; or do we act with the
soul as a whole in each of them once we are started? This will be
hard to determine in a way worthy of the argument. (436a-b)[8]

As the dialogue develops, especially in books 8–9, the option highlighted above (but undeveloped in book 4) is progressively elaborated.
The text between books 4 and 9, however, is not a box containing
nothing but a set of possible premises. The *Republic* is not a static argument. It is a dialectical work and thus much more like a conversation: it unfolds over time. The fact that Socrates does say something
different about the soul in book 9 than he does in book 4 is the result
of crucial developments in book 5, which force the tripartite psychology of book 4 *to be negated and revised*. On its own, the book 4 psychology *is* inadequate, and as I explain at length below, *it is meant to
be inadequate*. It represents a stage, a moment, of the dialogue and
not, as commentators too often refer to it, a "doctrine."

As Bobonich (1994) has shown, even if Socrates conceives of both
calculation and desire as themselves "agent-like" (he cites
437b1–c10, 439a1–d2, and 442b5–d1), the terrible dilemmas facing
the tripartite soul that Williams has uncovered still arise. Bobonich
states his objection this way: "The parts as conceived here, thus seem
to issue imperatives, e.g., 'Drink!' and 'Don't drink!' But the question
is: to whom are the imperatives addressed? . . . The most plausible
suggestion is that the conflicting imperatives are addressed to the
other parts." In other words, the "parts can communicate with one
another" (1994, 11–12). This option, however, "raises some problems
for Plato," implying, just as Williams has it, that what is "epithumetikon in a just soul harkens to the logistikon in that soul
through itself having an extra little logistikion of its own" (1997, 52).
In Bobonich's terms: "But now the Desiring part seems to have both
the original desires which conflicted with the judgment of the Reasoning part and an [all things considered] judgment that it is best to

8. Bloom imports the English "part" throughout this passage. In fact, *meros* is not
used and only pronouns appear. As usual, however, Bloom is consistent, and his translation very clear, so I retain it.

go along with the Reasoning part. Hence there is the possibility of conflict within the Desiring part" (1994, 12).

In other words, just as was represented in figure 1, if calculation and desire are both "agentlike"—that is, have desires and beliefs, which is the option Bobonich argues is both favored by the text and intrinsically more plausible—absurdity results. Plato is forced to "subdivide [the Desiring part] further"—that is, into calculation and desire—and as a result "will wind up with more parts of the soul than his theory allows for" (1994, 13, 14). In fact, he would wind up with an infinite number of parts. On the other hand, if Plato radically separates calculation from desire, then, as Annas (1982, 139) puts it, the latter is transformed into an "irrational, craving part" utterly incapable of hearkening to calculation's commands. Bobonich's final verdict is this: "A deep problem remains for Plato" (1994, 14).[9] To reiterate my response: this "deep problem" is implicit within the very notion of a soul containing distinct parts, and it is one Plato understands full well.

The crucial consequence of the "deep problem" is that if reason and desire are counted as distinct parts, then it becomes impossible to account for the passionate desire for wisdom— that is, for philosophy itself. At 435e, in articulating what Williams (1997, 51) calls the "whole-part rule," Socrates does mention "the love of learning" (*to philomathes*: 435e7), the same term he uses in book 9 (581b9). But given the meager resources of the tripartite scheme, which keeps desire far from reason, it is difficult to see how that scheme could possibly account for a desire to be reasonable. In contrast, by book 9, precisely such resources do become available. In other words, as Socrates himself suggests even here in book 4, *we act with the soul as a whole* rather than by means of three separate parts. *Pace* such critics as Williams and Bobonich, the inadequacy of the tripartite scheme is, as I explain at length below, a problem that Plato fully understands, overcomes, and integrates into later stages of the *Republic*.[10]

9. Bobonich (1994) believes that Plato improves the situation in the *Laws*.

10. Lear has addressed this from a very different and far more promising angle. Essentially, he accuses Williams of overly rigidifying Plato's psychology. Far from being a static structure, "Plato's is a developmental psychology" which offers "a dynamic account of the psychological transactions between inside and outside a person's psyche, between a person's inner life and his cultural enviroment" (Lear 1997, 61). In other words, the individual is not a self-contained psychological unit, not a "thing" as Penner (1990, 105) would have it. Instead, it is a dynamic being capable of both "internalizing" influences from the culture as well as "externalizing" itself and thereby helping to shape that culture. The result is a developmental process, not a static structure. Lear's proposal is similar to my own, and I return to it shortly.

The basic weakness of the tripartite psychology, the reason it is one-sided and thus inadequate, originates in the city-soul analogy itself. In order to make his task "easier," Socrates assumes that city and soul are like two isomorphic sets of letters: that is, two similarly structured, static wholes composed of discrete elements or units. In so assuming, he treats the soul arithmetically, as if it were an *arithmos*. (For the intimate link between numbers and letters, see Aristotle *Categories* 6.4b22.)

In ordinary Greek, *arithmos* means both "number" and "counting," and the former is never severed from the latter. As Martha Nussbaum explains, "The most general sense of *arithmos* in ordinary Greek of the fifth century would be that of an ordered plurality or its members, a countable system or its countable parts" (1979, 90). In Klein's words, a number is "a definite number of definite things" (1968, 46); for this reason, 0 and 1 are not *arithmoi*.[11] Given this understanding of *arithmos*, the tripartite soul of book 4 is clearly "arithmetical." Quite simply, it is conceived of as having countable parts.

An important indication of the arithmetical nature of the tripartite psychology is revealed in the highly formal argument Socrates uses to demonstrate that the soul has its first two parts, calculation and desire. To reiterate, it runs roughly thus:

Premise 1. The "Principle of Non-Opposition" (PNO): "the same thing won't be willing at the same time [*hama*] to do or suffer opposites with respect to the same part and in relation to the same thing" (436b).

Premise 2. Wanting (e.g., water) is opposite to not-wanting (water) (437c).

Conclusion. Therefore: "If ever something draws [the soul] back when it's thirsting, wouldn't that be something different in it from that which thirsts and leads it like a beast to drink?" (439b). The answer is yes. Therefore, two "forms in the soul" (439e) are distinguished: that which reasons and that which "loves, hungers, thirsts, and is agitated by other desires" (439d).

Decisive here is the temporal condition placed on the PNO by the Greek word *hama*, "at the same time." A thing can obviously suffer opposites at different times: I am now awake, but later I will be asleep. What is prohibited, of course, is my being both awake and

---

11. Wedberg (1955, 23) shows that Plato was not entirely consistent on this distinction. He cites *Laws* 818c and *Hippias Major* 302a.

asleep *at the same time*. The temporal condition implied by *hama* freezes what it governs. It rips a moment out of the flow of time. The conception of the soul generated by the PNO-dominated argument of book 4 is therefore of an atemporal or logical structure. Indeed, implied by the *hama*, and therefore implicit in all "truths" governed by the PNO, is the notion of timelessness or eternity. In this sense, what is governed by the PNO is similar to an *arithmos*, a static and intelligible, ordered plurality of discrete or countable parts.

Bernard Williams (1997) attacks this conception of the soul. But this conception is generated by assuming that the tripartite city is the soul written large: that is, is isomorphic with its three metallic classes. The isomorphism, however, cannot be maintained. Again, the diagram above clearly shows why. On the left side are the three classes of citizens, each of whom is an entire human being. On the right are "parts" of the soul. The two sides cannot be paralleled without generating Williams's absurdity. If desire is analogous to the working class, then either desire cannot obey orders because it is totally irrational, or, if it can obey orders it must be partially rational. But if it is the latter, then the transfer cannot be made to the desiring part of the soul without generating the infinite expansion of the number of "parts."

To reformulate again: an ordinary understanding of what it means to be human, which Socrates himself expresses later in the *Republic* (see 588e), obviously must feature rationality. As a result, the tripartite scheme leaves two equally unattractive implications. Either (1) there are totally irrational, and hence nonhuman, beings in the city and a totally irrational or nonhuman part in the soul, as well (in other words, there is something in "me" that is not "me"), or (2) the scheme suffers Bobonich's "deep problem" and Williams's "absurdity" that is, it generates an infinite expansion of "parts" within the soul.

Consider in more detail the manner in which Socrates treats desire in book 4. Just before launching into his analysis of it, he emphatically asserts that "each particular desire itself is only for that particular thing itself of which it naturally is, while the desire for this or that kind depends on additions" (437e). So, using thirst as his example, he insists that the object of thirst is not a hot or a cold or any other kind of drink; it is simply and only a drink. Socrates here anticipates an objection: "Let no one catch us unprepared . . . and cause a disturbance alleging that no one desires drink, but good drink, nor food but good food; for everyone, after all, desires good things" (438a).

Why would saying that "everyone desires good things" cause a disturbance? (Note that *thorubēsē* ["cause a disturbance"] at 438a1 is the same word Plato uses to express the reaction of the Athenian citizens to the trial of Socrates at 17d1 and 30c2 of the *Apology*). After all, doesn't Socrates himself occasionally say such things? (See 505e, for example.) Presumably, making such an assertion here would disrupt the structural integrity of the tripartite soul generated by the city-soul analogy. Desire is conceived of as a part of the soul distinct from calculation, whereas evaluation requires some measure of calculating. Socrates, then, seems intent on fending off this disturbance—the possibility of which he himself raises—with the following argument (which I paraphrase):

(1) The greater is greater than the less. The greater is greater than nothing other than the less, and the greater is not greater than itself.
(2) The much greater is much-greater than the much-less, the once-greater is once-greater than the once-less, and so on.
(3) In these sorts of quantitative relations, if X relates to Y, X relates only to Y and does so irreflexively.
(4) Housebuilding is knowledge only of constructing houses. It is not knowledge of anything else, nor is it knowledge of itself.
(5) Medicine is knowledge of health and sickness, and so on.
(6) Some knowledge X relates to its subject matter, Y.
(7) In all forms of knowledge, X relates only to Y and does so irreflexively.
(8) In all relations, X relates only to Y and does so irreflexively.
(9) Thirst is a relation, the desire for drink.
(10) Therefore, thirst is an irreflexive desire only for drink.

Because thirst is a desire only for drink, not for good drink, and because it is possible for a person both to want a drink and to resist drinking (on the grounds that it is not good to do so), *and because the PNO is at work*, there must be a second part of the soul—namely, calculation—which is responsible for the agent's resisting the drink.

Desire is here explicated via examples of quantitative relations and technical knowledge (housebuilding and medicine), each of which is construed as singular, unambiguous, and irreflexive (asymmetrical). In order to show just how one-sided these examples are, consider a similar list of relations found in the *Charmides*. There, too, while addressing the issue of self-knowledge, Socrates cites "greater than," "smaller than," "the double of," and other quantitative relations (168b–d) as his examples but includes such relations as seeing, hearing, and the rest of the senses (168c), and also desire, wish, love, fear, and opinion (168a–b). His purpose in offering this list is to cause trouble for the possibilty of self-knowledge: that is, for a specifically reflexive relation. When he concludes, however, Socrates says this: "In the various cases we have articulated, some strike us as absolutely impossible, while others raise serious doubts as to the faculty of the thing being ever applicable to itself. For with magnitudes, numbers and the like it is absolutely impossible" (168e).[12] But with others—including motion, a new addition to the list (168e)—he is noncommittal. It is, for example, manifestly possible to have an opinion of opinion, or to love love, and perhaps to desire desire. In short, certain psychological phenomena must be self-conscious and hence self-reflexive. Indeed, and of crucial significance for the *Republic*, philosophy itself must be one such psychological phenomenon. It demands reflection. It seeks to attain, for example, knowledge of knowledge and, of course, self-knowledge.

One last point about the *Charmides*: if the soul is conceived as being in self-motion, as it is in the *Phaedrus* (245c–e), and as it would be (at least on a metaphorical level) if the infinite expansion of the parts of the tripartite soul noted in the diagram above were to go into effect, then the addition of motion to the list above invites the reader to affirm the possibility of reflexive psychological relations.

In any case, I mention the *Charmides* list only to highlight by contrast how limited Socrates' examples of relations are in book 4 of the *Republic*: they are exclusively quantitative and technical. As a result, they generate a "digital" model of desire: X either wants Y—and if so, not necessarily a good Y, just Y—or does not want Y. There is no room for obscurity or complexity in this account of desire. Instead, it is exaggeratedly arithmetical. Socrates operates with such a model because he has a specific dialectical purpose in mind. It is he, after all, who initiated this entire train of thought by raising the potentially "disturbing" objection that someone might desire not a drink *simpliciter* but a good drink. He seems to raise this objection only in order to refute it. His goal seems to be to demarcate a strict boundary between calculation (which makes value judgments) and desire

12. This passage is taken from Walter Lamb's 1979 translation in the Loeb Classical Library.

(which is now conceived as without cognitive ability or, at least, without the cognitive ability to make value judgments) in order to parallel the relationship between the ruling and the working classes. But precisely by raising the objection, and then by presenting such a formal and abstract conception of desire, he also implies that the conception of the soul at work here is deficient. To reiterate the crucial case, the psychology of book 4 cannot account for the desire for wisdom—that is, for philosophy itself—which (as books 5 and 6 will make clear) requires the interpenetration of reason and desire, as well as self-reflection. (Nor can it account for any emotions, save anger, or for dreams or memory or repressed desires—in short, for a host of familiar psychological phenomena.) Nonetheless, for the several reasons I continue to develop throughout this chapter, it is useful for Socrates at this particular stage of the dialogue to present such an exaggeratedly arithmetical, such a "flat," conception of the soul.

To approach this same point from a different angle, consider Socrates' earlier treatment of the virtues. Note how he strangely avoids "moderation" (*sōphrosunē*). "How could we find justice so we won't have to bother about moderation any further?" (430d). Why is he so eager to skip moderation? Because this virtue threatens to disrupt the arithmetical picture of the soul. If moderation is conceived as a kind of self-control, then in exercising it, the agent becomes "stronger than himself." Such a phrase, though, is "ridiculous," because "the one who's stronger than himself would also be weaker than himself, and the weaker stronger" (430e). "Ridiculous," in this context, means self-contradictory or in violation of the PNO. (Note also that when Socrates summarizes the virtues at 441d, he pointedly leaves out moderation.)[13]

Moderation, the explicitly self-reflexive virtue, cannot be sustained, given the model of the soul operative in this discussion. But self-reflexion is manifestly a dimension of human, self-conscious life, as well as critical to philosophy itself. Therefore, the conception of the soul articulated in book 4 is inadequate. To supplement it, a psychological picture with "depth" is needed, one in which the soul acts upon itself while remaining itself: that is, it is not a static structure but a living being capable of a certain kind of self-motion. Subsequent developments in the *Republic*, particularly those in books 8 and 9,

13. Here I do not even mention the serious problem caused by the apparent overlap of moderation and justice.

provide just this. In fact, Socrates presents this very "image of the soul" at 588b–e. Here he radically revises the tripartite soul by describing an extremely strange creature. First, he instructs his listeners to draw a "single visible form [*idean*] for a many-colored, many-headed beast, that has a ring of heads of tame and savage beasts and can change them and make all of them grow from itself" (588c). This "manifold beast" (588e5) is the image of desire. Second, a lion tokens spirit. Third, in a striking but finally unsurprising move, Socrates asks that a human being represent reason. The final direction Socrates gives for completing the picture is this: "Then mold about them on the outside an image of one—that of the human being" (588d).

The picture Socrates asks us to "see" (*eidē*: 588b10) in fact cannot be seen. It is, just as Annas puts it (1982, 319), "visually incoherent" (in addition to being, as she says, "bizarre" and "slightly nightmarish"). Indeed, it is not a form, a "look," at all. A human exterior conceals within it a human being, a lion, and a many-headed beast. The human being within would presumably also contain a human being, a lion, and a many-headed beast. And so on. In other words, at the end of book 9, Socrates *affirms* precisely the infinite expansion of the parts of the soul that Williams and Bobonich so dread. This is a self-moving soul, a soul whose depth steadily increases. (Compare Heraclitus frag. 115: "The soul is a logos that increases itself.") The major task of this book is to explain how the dialogue reaches this nonpicture of the soul in book 9, and why it is more adequate, more truthful, than the tripartite, static one of book 4.

Despite its limitations, the psychology of book 4 is valuable, is positive, in at least three ways. (1) It discloses something important about our experience of ourselves. We often say, "My desire for chocolate got the better of me," or "My temper is out of control." The structural account of the soul—that is, the soul as viewed from the arithmetical perspective—offers an explanation of a way in which we, at least sometimes, ordinarily talk about ourselves. It is tempting and often useful to compartmentalize ourselves. It is, as the mere mention of "ego, id, and superego" suggests, almost irresistible to count ourselves as having three such parts. (2) In a similar fashion, dividing the city into three classes, one of which rules by reason and knowledge, helps us to consider the possibility that knowledge, and not merely opinion, should rule. It is crucial to ask why, how, and then (most important) *if* a city could actually be governed by a reasoned account of what is good for the whole, rather than by self-interested parts. (3) Because the argument generating the tripartite psychology is based on the PNO, which in turn is governed by the "at the same time" (*hama*) condition, it offers a conception of the soul that is in fact timeless. Nothing in "real life," in the empirical world, actually exists "at the same time." A being lives only in the flow of time, never in a single, frozen moment. To forbid the soul "to do or suffer opposites . . . at the same time" (436b) is, in this sense, irrelevant: because it is alive, the soul never exists "at the same time"; it is always moving. The psychology of book 4 rigidifies what is properly fluid.

On the other hand, this transformation of the living soul into a logical, timeless structure is deeply informative. It suggests that the timeless, the logical, does in fact intrude into human life. Human beings, as temporal and fluid as they may be, *can* gain some intellectual access to the eternal. For a variety of reasons, it is good and useful to realize this possibility, and the arithmetical is instrumental in teaching it.

The psychology of book 4 is inadequate nonetheless. It transforms one part of the soul, desire, into a non-soul, one part of me into a non-me. Even though it is often tempting, sometimes useful, and occasionally reassuring to think so, there is no non-soul in the soul, no non-me in me. (Nor are there any nonhumans among the human beings who reside in the city.) It is precisely to leave room for the reader to raise this objection that Plato, in introducing the tripartite psychology, has Socrates ask the crucial question, which I now cite for a second time.

> Do we act in each of these ways a result of the same part of ourselves, or are there three parts and with a different one we act in each of the different ways? Do we learn with one, become spirited with another of the parts within us, and desire the pleasures of nourishment and generation with a third; *or do we act with the soul as a whole in each of them once we are started?* This will be hard to determine in a way worthy of the argument. (436a–b; emphasis added)

The highlighted phrase shows Socrates himself raising the possibility that the soul does not act by means of three distinct parts. Instead, he wonders whether the whole is somehow "in each of them" (*kath hekaston autōn*: 436b1) whenever we start to act. Bloom's translation is problematic. First, Plato does not use the word "part" (*meros*); it does not appear until 442b11.[14] Second, without comment, Bloom translates *kath* as "in." In what sense, however, can the soul as a whole be "in" each of its parts in a psychological act? In fact, it was precisely by the whole being in each of the parts that, as Williams and Bobonich argue, the parts of the soul infinitely expand. Whatever *kath* exactly means, one point is certain: Socrates' question suggests the possibility of the soul's acting in a decisively nonarithmetical manner. After all, when it comes to numbers, a whole (say 12) is not "in" the parts (say 5 and 7). By contrast, Socrates suggests that in the act of learning, for example, or of philosophy itself, the whole soul and not simply calculation is somehow at work.

Robinson (1971) offers a similar reading of the passage. First, he emphasizes the ambiguity of Socrates' language. Although the argument seems to demonstrate that "there are more than one something or other in the soul," what is not clear is "more than one what?" (1971, 44). Calculation and desire, the two putative "somethings," cannot really be "parts," for " 'part' has a literal meaning only when it comes to spatially extended items," and "the soul occupies no space" (45). Perhaps then they are "kinds" or "forms": that is, *genē* (435b5, 441c6, 443d3) or *eidē* (435c1, 439e2). But these words, which are not used here in a technical or metaphysical sense, are too general to be informative. Therefore, Robinson retains the ambiguity of the passage by consistently using "something" to express Socrates' conclusion. Although more awkward than Bloom's, this translation is more accurate.

As Robinson notes, when Socrates spells out the two basic options—does the soul act by means of different parts or as a whole?—he actually "avoids the use of any nouns whatever" (46).[15] Instead, he opts for the instrumental dative (e.g., "that by which we learn"). Does this suggest that within the soul there are something like "tools?" Not according to Robinson:

> What we observe is always and only this or that mental act or experience or event . . . We know that from time to time we think and reason. And we know that from time to time we passionately

14. Thus, even though she is wrong in saying "*meros* is first used at 444b3," Annas is right about the more important point that instead of "part" Plato "uses more noncommital prepositional phrases which are clumsy in English, like 'that by which we desire' " (1982, 124).

15. Robinson (1971) consistently makes the mistake of saying "Plato" rather than "Socrates" here.

desire something. And we know that from time to time we think about our passionate desirings, and their consequences, and in our thoughts we sometimes reach practical decisions about our desirings, which we then carry out or do not carry out. And we find it very convenient to have nouns, "reason" and "desire," by which to refer to these events as if they were the work of some agents other than ourselves. . . . But in truth there is no agent here but ourselves. (1971, 47)

"Psychology," Robinson rightly says, "can have no anatomy of the soul" (47). Understood as an attempt to explain the life of the empirical soul, the argument leading to the tripartite scheme of book 4 is therefore unsound. "One and the same agent does do opposites at the same time. . . . Catullus both loves and hates Lesbia." Socrates' argument works "only if we interpret it as an analytic statement by using the 'with regard to the same,' *kata tauton*, to discount any and every actual opposition" (48).

The tripartite scheme cannot account for actual human experience. When we act, we (somehow) do so as a whole. On the other hand, dividing the soul into parts is, as Robinson puts it, often "convenient." I have already suggested what this might mean: it is useful to begin thinking of both city and soul as containing countable units. Furthermore, Socrates' argument is useful precisely because it is "analytic," or merely logical. Thinking of ourselves as timeless structures (note Robinson's repeated phrase "from time to time") gives us a taste of eternity. The tripartite scheme is inadequate nonetheless. In chapters 2 and 3, I explain how later stages of the *Republic*, especially books 8–10, contain an account of the soul far richer, far more faithful to human experience. Notably they do not do so in the form of a logical argument whose first premise is the PNO. Instead, Socrates tells some stories. He even alludes to this possibility at the end of the passage quoted above.

When faced with the question whether the soul acts via three "parts" or "as a whole," Socrates says, "This will be hard to determine in a way worthy of the argument (*logou*: 436b3)." But to what *logos* does he refer? Is it the conversation he has been engaged in with Glaucon and Adeimantus? If so, then "worthy of the *logos*" might mean "in keeping with the basic limitations of books 2–4." In other words, it might mean "excessively arithmetical."

Perhaps, however, "worthy of the *logos*" refers to the best possible philosophical account available. If so, then Socrates may well be pointing to the second option mentioned at 436a–b, that the soul works as a whole, not via three distinct parts. He anticipated just this sort of possibility when, in introducing the tripartite psychological scheme, he made this rather mysterious remark:

> But know well, Glaucon, that in my opinion, we'll never a get a precise grasp of [the soul] on the basis of procedures such as we're now using in the argument. There is another longer and further road leading to it. But perhaps we can do it in a way worthy of what's been said and considered before. (435d)

Again, there is more than one "road" or "way" to articulate the soul. The one being offered in book 4 is "worthy of," in keeping with, the PNO-dominated tripartite scheme developed via the city-soul analogy. There is, however, a longer, better, more complete, more satisfying, more truthful *logos* available. The psychology of book 4 is "worthy" only of what has been said before in books 2–4, in which an excessively arithmetical conception of city and soul have been generated. The longer road is one in which the authority of the PNO is dialectically overcome. It is one in which the *hama* clause is not invoked, and maintaining the structural integrity of the soul is not the primary objective. Instead, time is permitted to flow. It is a "road" in which, somewhat along the lines proposed by Jonathan Lear, the soul is seen as developmental and hence diachronic rather than as a static, letterlike structure with three distinct parts.[16] This later account, alluded to by Socrates' various comments discussed above, is supplied in the second and third waves of the *Republic*, especially in books 8 and 9, during Socrates' narrative of the "mistaken" regimes. There, via the medium of the story, he will be able to give just the kind of richer account of the soul that the limitations of the book 4 psychology clearly invite.

2. "THE ONE, THE TWO, AND THE THREE"

The psychology of book 4 is both "excessively arithmetical" and possessed of real, albeit limited, value. The latter description, as this section explains, emerges directly from the former. In other words, in the *Republic* the status or value of the arithmetical in general is consistently depicted as being intermediary. To elaborate, I discuss what Socrates in book 7 calls "the lowly [*phaulon*] business of distinguish-

16. See note 10.

ing the one, the two, and the three. I mean by this, succinctly, number and calculation" (522c). I begin with the opening of book 7, in which Socrates sketches what he calls an "image of our nature in its education and want of education" (514a). This, of course, is the allegory of the cave.

In the cave, there are shackled prisoners who are said to be "like us" (515a; see Smith 1997 for an extended discussion of this phrase). Because their heads are bound, they can face only the wall in front of them. On this wall images pass by. To the prisoners these seem real, but in fact they are only the shadows of various puppets, cast by the light of a fire. Education is the process of coming to see such shadows for what they really are: mere images of something more substantial. This requires, as Socrates indicates throughout this passage, a "turning around" (514b2, 515d3, 518c8, 518e4, 521c6) from image to reality. It all begins when the prisoner is released from the shackles, turns away from the shadows, and moves upward toward a vision of "things themselves" (515c–516a). Once released, the prisoners will presumably see, for example, the puppets that were responsible for producing the images at which they had stared for so long. Eventually, when fully out of the cave, they will see "the things in heaven and heaven itself." The final move or turn comes when the released prisoners see the highest object: that is, when they are able "to make out the . . . sun itself" (516a–b).

Upon completing his story of the cave, Socrates says, "This image as a whole must be connected with what was said before" (517b). He refers here to his discussion of the Idea of the Good, which he presented through its "offspring," the sun, and the divided line that closed book 6. In particular, he says the cave itself is like "the domain revealed through sight" (517b). This remark seems clearly to refer to the sensible realm depicted on the lower two portions of the divided line. The prisoner's journey from below the earth toward the sun is like the movement upward on the line toward the Idea of the Good (517c).

In general, then, the basic sense or "direction" of the three images is quite consistent. Each is divided into a higher and a lower, a superior and an inferior portion. The former is, roughly speaking, being or the intelligible; the latter is becoming or the sensible. In each of the three images, turning around—from earth to sun, sensible to intelligible, cave to sky—is the basic representation of philosophical education and progress.

Unfortunately, it is difficult to correlate precisely the terms of one image with those of another. Even if they are roughly analogous, it is impossible to know, for example, exactly how to use the divided line as a grid on which to map the items in (and out of) the cave. What segment of the line, for example, corresponds to the puppets casting the shadows in the cave? What about the puppeteers, or the fire in the cave, or the prisoners' shackles? Indeed, what are we to make of the pivotal role played by artifacts throughout the story? What about the stars and the moon that the released prisoner sees upon leaving the cave? To each question a plausible answer is easy to find but impossible to prove. The imagistic and hence necessarily elusive quality of sun, line, and cave cannot be totally eliminated.

Because the image of the cave is silent concerning the exact meaning of its specific elements, as well as its relationship to the divided line, and because it is intended to express something about the education of the "philosopher kings," Socrates supplements it with specific curricular proposals in book 7. Most important is the course of study meant to effect the pedagogically critical turning around of the soul from the sensible realm of becoming to the intelligible realm of being.

> Do you want us now to consider in what way such men [philosophers] will come into being and how one will lead them up to the light, just as some men are said to have gone from Hades up to the gods? . . . Then, as it seems this wouldn't be the twirling of a shell, but the turning of a soul around from a day that is like night to the true day; it is that ascent to what is which we shall truly affirm to be philosophy. (521c)

The specific study to effect this turning around is calculation and counting (*logizesthai te kai arithmein*: 522e2). In explaining why, Socrates offers a gloss on the divided line and, even more important, a fuller account of the intermediary status of the arithmetical. Some sensations, he says, are well suited to "summon," to call into play, the intellect. These are ones appearing to be self-contradictory. When looking at three fingers of a single hand, for example, the middle of the three may seem both larger and smaller. Reflection on this appearance quickly discloses why: the middle is larger than the smallest finger, and smaller than the largest. The intellect has been "summoned" in order to dissolve or stabilize a seeming contradiction (523b–524e; cf. 602d).[17]

---

17. See Nehamas 1975 for a good discussion of "the imperfection of the sensible world."

The most obvious and basic way the intellect does this kind of work is by measuring and counting. If I conceive of the three fingers as discrete units or individuals and determine that they are respectively, two, three, and four inches long, and then reconceive the three individuals as an ordered triad, the fact that the middle finger appears both larger and smaller no longer seems contradictory or troublesome in the least.

In this utterly ordinary (*phaulon*) act of organizing and counting, the soul is turned around. As mentioned above, an *arithmos* is an "ordered plurality" or "a definite number of definite things." It is a counting of items, of units. When I count three fingers on my hand, each finger functions as just such a unit. But the number "three" can also be used to count three toes on my foot. The same number is invoked to cover different sensible items. In fact, even in counting just three fingers, each unit is different from the other two. A moment's reflection, however, reveals that every count really treats, or transforms, its unequal sensible units, such as fingers, into equal units. As Klein (to whom much of this section is indebted) puts it, "Whenever we are engaged in counting, we substitute—as a matter of course, even if we are not aware of what we are doing—for the varied and always 'unequal' visible things counted 'pure' invisible units which in no way differ from each other" (1975, 117).

In other words, even the "vulgar" count of ordinary people (see *Philebus* 56d) invokes, and thereby implicitly gains access to, purely intelligible and completely stable entities: numbers. Simply to count, then, is uniquely and fundamentally informative. Much as the "at the same time" condition of the PNO offers a glimpse of the eternal, *arithmos* reveals how intelligible stability can and does intervene in human experience. There is something static and dry, something on which we can count, even amid the fluid mess, the "barbaric bog" (533d1), of human experience.

This is the crucial sense in which number turns the soul around, away from becoming to being. It is a compelling invitation to shift one's sights away from the sensible and toward the intelligible. Counting, the most ordinary of intellectual acts, "leads the soul powerfully upward" (525d6). Because it suggests the possibility of intellectual perfection, it can inspire us to think about other matters as well. Perhaps, for example, when it comes to questions of justice and injustice, there is something—call it the idea of justice—on which, like a number, we can utterly count. *Arithmos* gives us hope by supplying an ideal at which to aim. As Whitehead put it, "Our existence is invigor-

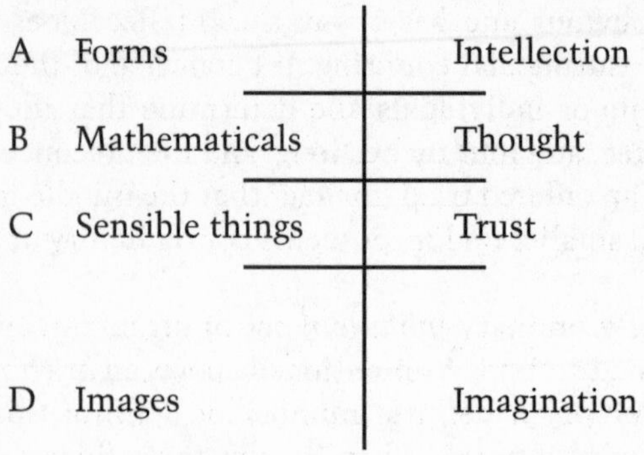

A	Forms	Intellection
B	Mathematicals	Thought
C	Sensible things	Trust
D	Images	Imagination

Figure 2

ated by conceptual ideals, transforming vague perceptions. . . . Here we find the essential clue which relates mathematics to the study of the good" (1971, 674).

As suggested above, the specific role to which Socrates assigns *arithmos* in his curricular proposals of book 7 functions as a gloss on the divided line. Before proceeding further, then, I begin a brief discussion of the line with a sketch (figure 2).

As shown, the line depicts both the objects of cognition, on the left, and the modes of cognition, on the right. So, when I see three fingers, I am in C, the realm of sensible objects, or simply "things." On the cognitive side, I am operating by means of "trust": that is, the most familiar mode of interacting with the world. Sensible experience, however, as the example of the fingers is meant to show, can often be less than trustworthy. It can seem self-contradictory. My second finger may seem both larger and smaller. When I measure it, however, I realize that it is three inches long and hence longer than two inches and shorter than four. In so doing, as I move upward to the "mathematicals"—in this case, number—the self-contradiction, the movement of perceptions over to their opposites, is replaced by arithmetic fixity. The numbers are pure and invariant, immune to change, indifferent to what sensible item they count and able to count them all. In this sense, they are "more real" than the things they are counting.[18] Hence, they are placed higher on the line.

Mathematics turns the soul from becoming to being because it transforms the sensible realm (C) into an image of, and so makes it

18. The notion of something being more real than something else is problematic.

dependent upon, an intelligible one (B). The "lowly" act of counting, available to virtually all human beings, testifies to this. The subsequent move from B to A, from the mathematicals to the Forms, and then the deployment of what is called "dialectic"—that is, of a power that makes "no use of anything sensed in any way, but using forms themselves, going through forms to forms, it ends in forms too" (511c)—is monumentally difficult to comprehend. I return to it later in this book (especially in the appendix). For the moment, suffice it to say that counting, the ordinary utilization of number, is the crucial intermediate step in the turning of the soul from the sensible world of becoming to the stable world of intelligible being: from C to B. For this reason, then, Socrates describes the mathematical disciplines as "assistants and helpers" (533d; also see 602d6). They are valuable, yes, but only in a limited and instrumental sense. They help to effect the turning around of the soul.

Because the mathematical is between the sensible and the higher reaches of the intelligible, it is possible for someone working in B to go either up or down. In fact, however, after having moved from C to B, from the sensible world to the mathematical/intelligible one, the human mind experiences a powerful force, a great temptation, to move back down again. This force is expressed best in the work of what Socrates calls the *technai*, the technical disciplines (511c; see Roochnik 1996 for an extended discussion). In an astonishing prefigurement of modern physics and the technology to which it gave birth, the divided line depicts technical knowledge as applied mathematics. Because the sensible world and the mathematicals fit together so well, the former is manipulable through the knowledge available in the latter. Counting and measurement are only the most obvious examples.

This unique relationship between the sensible and the mathematical is represented by the most salient visual (and geometrical) feature of the divided line: B and C are equal in length. This is especially striking because the few directions Socrates gives for constructing the line (at 509d) are, with this one exception, ambiguous. It is not apparent, for example, whether it should be vertical or horizontal. (Only some remarks Socrates makes later, at 511a and 511d, suggest the latter. See Smith 1997 for a thorough discussion.) Socrates does not say whether the modes of cognition should be placed on the left or the right side. Most perplexing is the question of whether segment A or D is the longer. My version above suggests D, but there is no way of proving it correct. By the sharpest possible contrast, what can be proved is the exact equality of B and C (see Klein 1975, 119). This equality symbolizes the uniquely perfect fit between the sensible and the mathematical realms. The book of nature, as the Pythagoreans intuited and as modern physics has so thoroughly elaborated, is written in the language of mathemetics.

The utter clarity with which the equality of B and C is depicted represents a fundamental tendency of human thought. Because they fit so well, because mathematical knowledge is so amazingly useful in the sensible world, it is always tempting to submit to the force of "intellectual gravity," to apply mathematical knowledge to the sensible realm—that is, to engage in the *technai*. Technical thinking, in ancient Greece and on the Internet, is always a lure and therefore invites itself to be regarded as the paradigmatic form of knowledge itself. The goal of philosophical education, however, is to resist this lure.

Socrates makes the point by referring to the items in B—"the odd and the even, the figures, three forms of angles" (510c)—as "hypotheses." As usual, what this means is much debated. For the moment, consider only the word's etymology, which is crucial to Socrates' use of it here. "Hypothesis" literally means "that which is placed under." Those who move downward from B to C by, say, applying the 3-4-5 right triangle to a work of carpentry—that is, by being technical—actually distort the real status of the mathematical items in B: instead of placing them below, they treat those items as if they were higher entities that need only to be applied. By contrast, the philosopher, the soul who turns around, treats the hypotheses as what they really are: something placed under, "not [as] beginnings but [as] really hypotheses—that is, steppingstones and springboards—in order to reach what is free from hypothesis at the beginning of the whole" (511b).

The passage is much contested, and once again I eschew detailed analysis. What is central here is only this: technical thinking seems to be a natural inclination of human thinking. First, one moves from C to B—that is, one counts or measures—and then, after thoroughly familiarizing oneself with the items in B, moves back down to C. Human beings learn a bit of mathematics and then apply it profitably to the "real world" where it is so stunningly useful. They commute between the exactly equal segments of B and C. However useful this mode of thinking may be, it actually confuses what is intermediary with what is genuinely high. It treats mathematics as the pinnacle of thought, not as a stepping-stone. The *technai* are best utilized, as Socrates puts it, as "assistants and helpers," not as the final achievement of human cognition. In other words (and as Socrates consistently says elsewhere), their value is real but limited. (See Roochnik 1994 for a discussion of the other dialogues in which this view is expressed.)

The rigidly controlled curriculum of book 7 of the *Republic* is designed to train the guardians to resist the temptation to move from B down to C. They are not allowed to study mathematics "in the fashion of private men, but to stay with it until they come to the contemplation of the nature of numbers with intellection itself, not practicing it for the sake of buying and selling like merchants or tradesmen" (525c). Despite the powerful usefulness of mathematics, the guardians of Kallipolis are forced to defy intellectual gravity and to move upward to "the nature of numbers" themselves as a prelude to their study of the Forms. Again, it is far from clear what this specifically means, but one item is certain: education is a turning around, from C to B and then from B to A; from the sensible to the mathematical and then to an even higher plane of the purely intelligible Forms.

Socrates says that *arithmos* is

the lowly business . . . of distinguishing the one, the two, and the three. I mean by this succinctly, number and calculation. Or isn't it the case with them that every kind of art and knowledge [*epistēmē*] is compelled to participate in them? (522c)

All *technai* and *epistemai* (the two words can here be counted as synonyms) participate in number. It is not quite clear what this means. In what sense does the description hold for, say, medicine? The key, as I have argued at length elsewhere (Roochnik 1996), lies in an essential feature of a *technē*; it has a determinate subject matter; it is about a single area. The man with the *technē*, the *technitēs*, is an expert whose expertise is limited to the specific field in which he is knowledgeable. Furthermore, the subject matter of a *technē* can be internally divided and organized. Medicine, for example, is a single area of expertise but is composed of several subdivisions: anatomy, nutrition, pharmacology, and so on. Because it can be analyzed into its component elements, *technē* is the paradigmatically teachable form of knowledge. It is clear, reliable, and usually productive of some useful result. In all these senses, then, *technē* shares features with the arithmetical. This, I believe, is the reason why Socrates says that every techne is compelled to participate in the one, the two, and the three—that is, in *arithmos*.

The entire first wave of the *Republic*, which I have been describing as excessively arithmetical, might thus equally as well be described as excessively technical. This is most apparent in the first step Socrates takes in the founding of Kallipolis. He begins with a very simple city, one composed of only a few men who are "in need of much" (369b). In order for this "city of utmost necessity" (369d) to function well, labor must be divided. There must be (at least) a farmer who supplies food for the others, a housebuilder, a weaver, and a shoemaker. Furthermore, since "different men are apt for the accomplishment of different jobs," and since one man practicing "one art" will do "a finer job" than "one man practicing many arts," each of these technicians must strictly specialize. Socrates then formulates what turns out to be a guiding principle for the entire city: "one man, one *technē*" (370b). In book 4, when he is searching for justice, this is precisely the principle Socrates re-invokes: "Each one must practice one of the functions in the city." This is the background assumption that leads to the definition of justice as "the minding of one's own business and not being a busybody" (433a). If everyone in the city does his job, performs his *technē*, the city will function smoothly.

Socrates' statement of the basic principle "one man, one art" is more striking in Greek than in English. It is simply *mian heis* (370b5) or, literally, "one one." (Because the first "one" is feminine accusative, it clearly modifies the *technēn* implicit at 370b5; the second "one," in the masculine nominative, refers to the *tis* at 370b4.) *"One one" works well as the very motto of Kallipolis*. It is a city in which citizens are transformed into units. Each belongs to one of the three classes and performs a single task. Kallipolis as a whole is meant to operate with technical precision.

In sum, from the way Socrates explains and conceives of *arithmos* and *technē* in book 6 of the *Republic*, it is clear that both have an inflated status in the building of Kallipolis in books 2–4. In other words, the first wave of the *Republic* finds the arithmetical being treated not as a hypothesis placed "under" thinking, to be used as a springboard upward (from B to A on the divided line), but as a conceptual end in itself which needs only to be applied (from B to C). This is the great limitation of the first wave, which culminates in the tripartite psychology of book 4.

As repeatedly stated, *arithmos*, even if only intermediary, has significant epistemic and practical value. So too, therefore, does the arithmetical picture of city and soul. It is useful, even illuminating, to think of the soul as having distinct parts. When Leontius wants to see the corpses, tells himself to resist, fails, and then reprimands himself by screaming at his eyes, "Look, you damned wretches" (440a), his experience can be usefully described by dividing his soul into three parts: his desire to look, his calculation that it is wrong to look, and his spirited anger at himself. But the value of such a tripartition is limited. There is no entity in Leontius's soul called "desire" radically separate from another entity called "calculation." There is no non-Leontius in Leontius. Instead, he is somehow acting with his "soul as a whole" (436b), and as a result the arithmetical structure must be violated. Still, it is useful and proper to begin thinking about the soul as tripartite. Doing so sheds light. But to give in to the temptation of conceiving of ourselves as numberlike objects and therefore as material for technical manipulation would be a grave mistake. Indeed, this is precisely the mistake made by the rulers of Kallipolis, the city of units. They attempt to calculate a "marriage number" that will give them the power to control human reproduction (see 546a–547a). Their failure to achieve this power is one of the most pivotal moments in the *Republic*, and I return to it below.

The same point about the value of the arithmetical holds for cities. It is useful to begin thinking about the city as as having three metallically rigid kinds of citizens—gold, silver, and bronze—each of whom performs one and only one task. Doing so brings into sharp focus the possibility of a ruling class that governs by the authority of knowledge rather than by force or opinion. This notion is, on the one hand, profoundly appealing and hopeful. Surely there are few political spectacles as demoralizing as that of the ignorant pandering to the even more ignorant. But on the other hand, as developments throughout the dialogue are meant to show, rule by a knowledgeable few is also dangerous and potentially noxious, for it might transform one class of human beings into irrational nonhumans who need only to receive orders. To cite the most egregious example: in the name of solidifying their authority, the rulers of Kallipolis decide to send "all those in the city who happen to be older than ten . . . out to the country" (540e). In other words, in order to produce a clean slate of new citizens uncontaminated by the ignorance infecting the previous regime, the Kallipolean guardians must exile everybody older than ten.

A third way in which the arithmetical can be construed as useful is as a rhetorical, or therapeutic, device. The best example comes from the *Gorgias*. Socrates is trying to reform the remarkably ambitious Callicles, whom he diagnoses as suffering from *pleonexia*, the desire to have more than one's fair share. For Socrates, the etiology is simple. He says to Callicles, "You hold that *pleonexia* is what one ought to practice, for you disregard geometry" (508a). Socrates urges Callicles to replace his chaotic striving after political power with a vision of a cosmos, a stable, orderly, intelligible world, to which mathematics offers the best invitation. In terms of the divided line, he exhorts Callicles to turn around, away from C to B and then to A. For doing so, mathematics is instrumental. It is useful in shifting the sights and redirecting the ambitions of a potential tyrant. Since Glaucon shares, to some extent, Callicles's spiritedness, it may well be that Socrates consistently exaggerates the arithmetical in the early books of the *Republic* in order to benefit him (see Roochnik 1994 for an elaboration).

To close: the arithmetical is a useful place to begin but a bad place to end. It must be treated as inspiring rather than paradigmatic. As a result, to describe Kallipolis as excessively arithmetical is to ready it for dialectical negation. This is why the *Republic* does not terminate with book 4. To explain and defend this notion further, as well as to prepare better for the key transition taking place at the outset of book 5, the next section describes in more detail the arithmetical quality of Kallipolis.

3. THE ARITHMETICAL CHARACTER OF KALLIPOLIS

In constructing his city in books 2–4, Socrates aims to endow it with two principal attributes: stability and unity, both pivotal features of the arithmetical. To achieve his goals, Socrates focuses first on the systematic control of education. From their youth, the citizens of Kallipolis must be prepared to assume and abide by their functions in the city. Socrates begins with "music," by which he means the literary culture that becomes the shared background of the citizens: "First, as it seems, we must supervise the makers of tales" (377b). Poetry, understood in a sense broad enough to encompass all kinds of storytelling, must be censored.

By putting strict laws in place, Socrates addresses both the form and the content of Kallipolean poetry. When he has finished, he then implements a blanket prohibition against innovation.

For they [the guardians] must beware of change to a strange form of music, taking it to be a danger to the whole. For never are the ways of music moved without the great political laws being moved. (424c)

Socrates begins with "Kallipolean mythology," those stories of the gods that circulate in the city. How the gods are depicted in myths, he seems to assume, will have a direct impact on the formation of the citizens. Consider the following seven points.

(1) The story of Cronos's fight against and ultimate castration of Uranus, as presented in Hesiod, must be suppressed (378a). The rationale, of course, is that telling such a tale to a young person might implicitly countenance the citizens' doing similar deeds to their own fathers. What is needed in Kallipolis is stability and unity. Citizens must accept the authority of the rulers, and in general, young people must be tempted by no form of rebellion. In this spirit, then, Kallipolis prohibits all assaults on and dishonoring of elders (465a).

(2) "It mustn't be said that gods make war on gods" (378c). Again, the rationale is obvious. If gods are shown to be fighting each other, so too would fights among citizens be implicitly sanctioned. Socrates' objective is to use poetry to inculcate the belief "that no citizen ever was angry with another, and that to be so is not holy" (378c).

(3) Kallipolean myths must depict the gods as the cause of only good things. Socrates presents something of an argument for this point.

(a) A god is "really good" (379b).
(b) Therefore, a god is not harmful.
(c) That which is not harmful does no "harm" or "evil" (379b). "The good is not the cause of everything, rather it is the cause of the things that are in a good way, while it is not responsible for the bad things" (379b).
(d) Therefore, a Kallipolean god, "since he's god, wouldn't be the cause of everything" (379c) but only of good things.
(e) Therefore, "we mustn't accept Homer's . . . foolishly making this mistake about the gods and saying that, 'Two jars stand on Zeus's threshold / Full of dooms—the one of good, / the other of wretched.' . . . Nor that Zeus is the dispenser to us, 'Of good and evil alike'" (379d–e).

Socrates defends this stricture by saying that a mythology so regulated would be "advantageous for us" (380c), presumably because citizens could not then take their bearings from gods who cause evil: that is, gods who are not utterly reliable. For similar reasons, a Kallipolean god cannot be said to lie: "The god is altogether simple and true in deed and speech" (382e).

(4) A Kallipolean god never changes at all but, "remains forever simply in his own shape" (*morphē*: 381c9). To borrow a word from the *Symposium* (211b), a god is "monoeidectic," having one and only one form. In defense of this notion, Socrates offers what is now familiar to us as some sort of theological argument. I paraphrase as follows:

(a) If X "steps out of its own intelligible form," it is changed either by itself or by something else (380e).[19]
(b) The better X is, the less X is changed by external forces (380e).
(c) The gods are in the best condition (381b).
(d) Therefore, the gods are not changed by external forces.
(e) If the gods change, the change is caused internally (381b).
(f) Since the gods lack nothing, if the gods change, they can only get worse. But gods would not willingly make themselves worse.
(g) Therefore, gods do not change internally.
(h) Therefore, gods do not change at all.

Numerous presuppositions are at work in this argument, and a thorough analysis could easily turn up all sorts of problems. What is most important here is only this basic theme: Kallipolean gods are self-identical units. In other words, they are as dry as numbers. As paradigms in the official mythology of the city, they are designed to inculcate similar attributes in the citizens, to make them stable, reliable, and resistant to change. In this regard, consider some further features of Kallipolean poetry.

(5) When it comes to the "official eschatology," poets are not allowed "to disparage Hades' domain" (386b). As opposed to the extraordinarily bitter lament of the dead Achilles in the *Odyssey* (386c), or Homer's poignant description of the hopeless shadows in Hades, in Kallipolis "a decent man will believe that for the decent man . . . being dead is not a terrible thing" (387d). The fear of death can cause men to behave in unpredictable ways. Notably, it can lead them to break ranks during a battle. Fear of death must be eliminated because it destabilizes the political order by elevating the individual's inter-

19. Bloom retains "idea" in this passage.

ests above those of the city. To this end, wailing over fallen comrades and excessive lamentation over the dead (388b–c) are prohibited.

(6) In Kallipolean poetry, good will always triumph over bad. Poets will be forbidden to say "that many happy men are unjust and many wretched ones just, and that doing injustice is profitable if one gets away with it, but justice is someone else's good and one's own loss" (392b). Once again, the objective is to inculcate within the citizens, by means of the paradigms that are impressed upon them by the "musical" culture in which they are nourished, a sense of the importance of continually doing what is right. (Strikingly, however, Glaucon himself violates this stricture by telling the ring of Gyges story [359c–360b], which itself is the impetus of the very project of building Kallipolis.)

(7) A minor point is the elimination of raucous comedy from the Kallipolean repertoire. The citizens should not be "lovers of laughter either. For when a man lets himself go and laughs mightily, he also seeks mighty change to accompany his condition" (388e). In other words, those who laugh hard let down their guard and thereby become vulnerable. He who laughs hard is open, and Kallipolis is the most closed and serious of cities, one in which all citizens must obey the rulers and exhibit self-control (389e). It is, of course, a city in which citizens are not permitted to lie (389b).

Socrates' strictures reach down to the particulars of style. Kallipolean poetry, for example, is allowed to be like the Homeric epics insofar as they can mix narration and imitation (396e). But, unlike Homer, it permits only an "imitation of the decent" (397d). (That this stricture is revised in book 10, where all imitation is prohibited, is addressed in the third section of chapter 3.) Even more detailed is the supervision of what in English is simply called "music." For example, only the Dorian and Phrygian modes are retained (399a). The flute, the instrument of the god of wine and fluidity (namely, Dionysus), is out, whereas the lyre and cither, instruments associated with the god of clarity and individuation (Apollo), are in (399d).

The foregoing brief observations only underscore the obvious. Kallipolean culture is tightly regulated, and its goal is consistently to produce reliable citizens. To reiterate, once its strictures are firmly in place, they are not allowed to change.

In explicitly political terms, the essential purpose of Kallipolean legislation is to end factionalism. "Have we any greater evil for a city than what splits it and makes it many instead of one?" Socrates asks (462a8–b2). The answer is no (cf. 444b). "That city in which most say 'my own' and 'not my own' about the same thing, and in the same way" (462c), is the best governed city. The "noble lie," introduced in book 3 (414d–e), is specifically designed to inhibit the growth of factions and instill a sense of common purpose in the citizens. (Faction, of course, does arise and ultimately causes the breakdown of Kallipolis: see 545d.)

The noble lie has two distinct parts: the autochthonous nature of citizens (414d) and the three metals (415a). (Again, I collapse bronze and iron into one category.) The purpose of both is clear. Believing that they are autochthonous, the citizens will consider the city itself to be their mother (414e2) and their fellow citizens to be siblings. As a result, they will become patriots (from *patēr*, "father"), willing to subordinate and even to sacrifice their lives in defense of the city. Believing their psychological makeup to be as rigid and fixed as metal, Kallipoleans will accept their stratum in the city as a matter of natural necessity. This acceptance will inculcate stability by defusing the possibility of discontent, factionalism, and rebellion. Socrates' justification of the lie seems consequentialist: it is permissible to lie to the citizens because increasing the level of patriotism and political stability brings great benefit to the city.

Socrates adds an important caveat when he closes his discussion of the lie: "God commands first and foremost to be of nothing such good guardians and to keep over nothing so careful a watch as the children, seeing which of these metals is mixed in their souls" (415b). If a bronze-souled child is born to a gold parent, the child must be turned over to the "craftsmen or the farmers" (415c).

This is exceptionally strong language. Nothing, says Socrates, is more important to Kallipolis than control of Eros, because Eros privatizes, personalizes, and destabilizes. Eros makes me love her rather than you, care more about my children than I do about yours. Eros makes me want you or this or that and care more about getting what I want than about what I should be doing on behalf of the city. Eros is the limb-loosener and always threatens to interrupt, to tyrannize, to lay waste the best of rational plans. The noble lie has human beings falling naturally into three metallic types and is justified on the grounds that maintaining the tripartite structure of the city is of utmost importance. The lie assumes that Eros can be controlled.

Socrates takes this legislation of the erotic one crucial step further.

To maintain the tripartite structure, "the possession of women, marriage, and procreation of children must as far as possible be arranged according to the proverb that friends have all things in common" (423e). Only the elimination of the family will ensure full identification of all citizens with the city. As the noble lie puts it, the city, not any private citizen, must be construed as the parent.

In general, much of the Kallipolean educational program, culminating in the noble lie, can be expressed in terms of the control of Eros. The goal is the rearing of disciplined young people who hate the ugly (402a) and love only the fine (402d)—that is, the politically advantageous. In sum, "musical matters should end in love matters [*ta erōtika*] that concern the fair" (403c6–7).

The noble lie prefigures a later development in the *Republic*: namely, the marriage number that Socrates announces in book 8. Despite the fact that "a city so composed [Kallipolis] is hard to be moved" (546a), it does fall apart. This happens because "although they are wise, the men you educated as leaders of the city will nonetheless fail to hit on the prosperous birth and barrenness of your kind with calculation aided by sensation" (546b). The guardians will fail to calculate accurately the notoriously obscure "marriage number." Whatever this mysterious number may be, it represents the key to a mathematically based eugenics. Because the rulers fail to find it, citizens "will at some time beget children when they should not." The result will be "the chaotic mixing of iron with silver and of bronze with gold" (547a). From this will arise the dreaded disease of the just city: namely, "faction."

As is explained further in chapter 2, the failure of the guardians to calculate the marriage number in book 8 represents the moment of the dialogue "in which the forces of mathematics are invaded by the forces of appetite" (Geertz 2000, 50). Simply put, the former cannot control the latter, and so Kallipolis disintegrates. This "invasion," however, is prefigured in the noble lie. It is, after all, a lie. Presumably, then, Kallipoleans are not actually demarcated into gold, silver, and bronze classes. They are not born from the earth. They are private as much as they are public beings. Their souls are fluid, not metallic. They are erotic.

As suggested above, the arithmetical character of Kallipolis can be traced back to its origin. Taking the first step toward an exposition of political justice in book 2, Socrates constructs a small city arising from the need (369b5) that citizens have for one another:

One man takes on another for one need and another for another
need, and, since many things are needed, many men gather in one
[*pollous eis mian*] settlement as partners. (369c1–3)

The language is that of arithmetic: many units are summed into
one. This implies, of course, that the units must be countable, and indeed the first city is said to be "made of four or five men" (369d). (See
Page 1995 on why Socrates vacillates here.) The city is strictly organized around the motto "one one," the principle of "one man, one
art" (370b2), and achieves a minimal level of efficiency in order to
meet the basic needs of the small (and, at least initially, seemingly
only male) population.[20] It is a peaceful city with a stable population.
On this last point Socrates says, "They will have sweet intercourse
with one another, and not produce children beyond their means"
(372b9; cf. 509b9). In other words, their Eros will not spin out of control. The problem is, as Glaucon points out, that Socrates' first city is
"without relishes" (372c2).[21] It does not satisfy those citizens whose
desires, exceeding the basic, are expansive and powerful. Thus, says
Glaucon, such a city is fit only for pigs (372d4). With this crucial objection comes the all-important transition from Socrates' "true" and
"healthy" city (372e6) to Glaucon's "luxurious" (372e3) and "feverish" one (372e8).

This second city, unlike the first, is realistically infused with unnecessary human desires. In the feverish city there are not only relishes but also perfume, incense, courtesans, and cakes. It contains
painting and embroidery, poetry, music, beauticians, barbers, and
cooks. The full gamut of human desire, from sex to art, flourishes in
the city Glaucon's interruption inspires (373a–c).

This list tokens what is missing from the city of pigs—Eros. The
citizens of Socrates' first city are conceived as simple units who can
be counted on to perform their *technē*. But in a real city there are, for
example, no shoemakers *simpliciter*; instead, there are human beings

20. Even though it is supposed to be a city of "utmost necessity" (369d), this first
city produces a sufficient surplus of goods to be exported. Hence, there are merchants
(371a). This is actually a significant fact, for it shows the lie implicit in the first city:
namely, that it is utterly stable.

21. *Opson* can mean "roasted meat" as well as "relish." Meat-eating is an important symptom of the first city's feverishness, as well as the cause of its need to expand.
See 559b, 582c8, 585b for additional examples. Eating in general pops up throughout
the dialogue (e.g., 496c); philosophy tastes sweet (490b6); and the philosopher is nourished on being (582c8 and 585b). Finally, note that despite the promise of dinner (328a),
no food is actually served during the *Republic*.

who make shoes, raise families, go to the Assembly, and sometimes cause trouble. In other words, and as Glaucon realizes, real people are not like numbers, nor are their souls metallic.

Because it is energized by the indefinite expansion of human desire, the feverish city will itself expand and invade its neighbors to meet the increasing demands of its own citizens (especially for meat: 373c). As a result, there will be war. Socrates is strikingly ambivalent about this development: "And let's not yet say whether war works evil or good" (373e). Since the principle of "one man, one art" is operative, there must be a warrior class. Those who are to fight on the city's behalf must be fast and strong, but most of all they must be "spirited": quick to anger, loving of victory, and ready to fight (375a–b). Such warriors are needed if the city is to expand successfully, but their presence in the city poses a grave problem: "How will they not be savage to one another and the rest of the citizens?" (375b). The initial legislation of Kallipolis, all of which concerns education, is meant to address just this problem. These guardians must be educated to be "gentle to their own and cruel to enemies" (375c1)—in short, to identify their interests with those of the city. To reiterate, *the* problem Kallipolis is meant to resolve, and thus the problem of political philosophy itself, is precisely the socialization of those citizens who have spirit and desire more than is necessary.

Just as his reaction to the onset of war is ambivalent, so too is Socrates' judgment of the first and second cities. Despite the appellation "true" and "healthy," it is far from obvious whether he actually prefers the first, "most necessary," city over its feverish descendant. In other words, as the example of Theages (496b–c) is later meant to suggest, health is not always a self-evident good. Consider the following comment Socrates makes about the Glaucon-inspired city:

> All right, I understand. We are, as it seems, considering not only how a city, but also a luxurious city, comes into being. Perhaps that's not bad either. For in considering such a city too, we could probably see in what justice and injustice naturally grow in cities. (372e)

On the one hand, Kallipolean music is designed to "purge" (399e) the feverish city and thus restore it to the health and stability of Socrates' first city. (For this reason, of course, Kallipolis dispenses "drugs" that is, its rulers tell the pharmaceutically noble lie [382c, 414c].) On the other hand, unlike the first city, the second is realistic, for only in it are present the uniquely human desires for extravagance, beauty, and unnecessary sex. On the one hand, Kallipolean legislation is meant to cure the fever and to restore the stability found in the city of pigs. On the other hand, the basic strategy for accomplishing this stability—namely, to abide by the motto of "one one," organizing the city in strictly arithmetical terms—is profoundly problematic. For the impetus of "one one" generates the tripartition of the soul and animates the psychology of book 4, whose account of desire is generated by an argument governed by the PNO (and its "at the same time" condition).

To close this chapter, I again refer to the essay "Plato's Theory of Desire" by Charles Kahn, who repeatedly stresses that the "Platonic conception of reason is a form of desire" (1987, 80). As he puts it, reason is responsible for learning, and "nothing could cause us . . . to learn if it did not make us want to learn" (81). As cited above, ultimately he defines reason as "essentially desire for the good" (84). Like several other commentators mentioned in this chapter's first section, Kahn reverts to passages from later books of the *Republic* in order to make his point. But unlike them, he at least gestures toward an explanation of why such a move might be justified: a "fuller psychology" (86) is available in books 8 and 9, because "Plato could not present his full-strength conception of the rule of reason in Book 4, before the appearance of philosophy" (88). He further differentiates "Plato's account of pre-philosophical virtue in *Republic* 4 and the account of philosophical virtue in Books 5–6" (87).

In other words, Kahn understands that the dialogue has made progress, that it is dialectical in character, and that as a result the tripartite psychology of book 4 is not Plato's last word. Unfortunately, he does not methodically develop this line of thought. He does not ask, for example, *why* philosophy appears only after book 4—even though, in fact, he has his finger on the answer. Kahn understands that book 9.581, the passage which so many commentators refer to in order to bring back together the fragmented soul of book 4, is essentially dependent on Eros. Here each part of the soul is renamed and reconceived: "wisdom-loving, victory-loving, gain-loving" (581c) replace calculation, spirit, desire. The soul is unified via Eros.[22] As

---

22. At 581c the Greek for "loving" is expressed in the prefix *philo*. This raises the issue of the relationship between *philia* and Eros. I do not see a sharp distinction between them in this context, but see Hyland 1968.

Kahn puts it, Eros is "an undifferentiated source of psychic energy or motivation for all 3 parts" (96). To explain, he relies on a crucial passage from book 6:

> But, further, we surely know that when someone's desires incline strongly to some one thing, they are themselves weaker with respect to the rest, like a stream that has been channeled off in that other direction. . . . So, when in someone they have flowed toward learning and all that's like it, I suppose they would be concerned with the pleasure of the soul itself with respect to itself and would forsake those pleasures that come through the body. (485d)

Here is a "hydraulic model" of desire to contrast with the static and dry structure of book 4. Kahn likens it to Freudian sublimation and cites *A General Introduction to Psychoanalysis*: libidinal impulses "are related to one another like a network of communicating canals filled with fluid." So Eros, on this view, is "a common pool of motivational energy" (1987, 97).

Kahn is on to something important. As the first section of chapter 2 explains, Eros is the great interruption of the *Republic*. When Polemarchus and Adeimantus, and then Glaucon and Thrasymachus, "arrest" (450a) Socrates at the beginning of book 5, they force him to address Eros. Specifically, they demand that he elaborate the "community of children and women," his proposal to destroy the family and its private erotic attachments. At precisely this moment the tripartite, arithmetical, and dry conception of the soul articulated in book 4 begins to give way. As Socrates puts it, when Eros intrudes, a troubling, swarming, expanding *logos* is set in motion (450a). The second two waves of the dialogue, books 5–7 and especially books 8–10 are this *logos*.

Despite being alert to both the developmental character of the dialogue and the powerful role Eros plays, Kahn finally shies away from his own insight; speaking of the hydraulic model of desire, he doubts "whether this view of Eros can be attributed to Plato," because it "would do nothing to account for the radical divergence of the three parts" (1987, 98). Unfortunately, like so many commentators, Kahn remains fixated on the tripartite soul.

The tripartite psychology of book 4 is generated on the basis of the city-soul analogy that Socrates offers in book 2 as a way of making his task "easier." As Williams (1997) and Bobonich (1994) have shown, it is inadequate. It is so because it is one-sided and partial, because it is excessively arithmetical. As such, it is fully in keeping with the entire character of books 2–4. In this, the first wave of the dialogue, Socrates constructs a city composed of unitary citizens whose sole purpose is to exercise well their *technical* function. Citizens belong to a single class and, guided by the myth of the metals as well as the entire Kallipolean musical program, conceive of themselves as static beings incapable of change. Eros is strictly controlled—or so, at least, it seems.

But this wave of the *Republic* is only the first of three. Just as at the beginning of book 2, Glaucon interrupted Socrates when he thought he was "freed from [his] argument" (357a) with Thrasymachus, and just as Glaucon destroyed the peaceful city of pigs when he demanded his "relishes" (372c), so too will Socrates be interrupted a third time at the beginning of book 5. He is not, in fact, done with Kallipolis—although he claims to wish he were—because Eros has not been given its due.

CHAPTER TWO

Eros

I. INTIMATIONS OF EROS

Eros enters the *Republic* covertly and early on.[1] But its impact, as always, is strong. Socrates has been "forced" to stay in the Piraeus and to visit the home of Polemarchus (327b–c). There he meets the paterfamilias, the wealthy arms merchant and metic Cephalus. He greets Socrates with a studied warmth and claims that if he weren't so old, he would make the trip to town more often.

> As it is, however, you must come here more frequently. I want you to know that as the other pleasures, those connected with the body, wither away in me, the desires and pleasures that have to do with speeches grow the more. (328d)

Cephalus's desires are "withering away," and only because they are now dormant is he open to the pleasures of conversation. Socrates welcomes the opportunity to talk with Cephalus, for he is, he says, eager to know "what sort of road" (328e) old age is. He is asking, in other words, the strangely intrusive question "What's it like to be close to death?" Cephalus is glad to answer. He boasts of being quite different from most of his agemates. They lament the passing of their youth, when they frolicked in sex, drinking, and feasts (329a). Cephalus, by admirable, albeit self-described, contrast, agrees with old Sophocles.

> I was once present when the poet was asked by someone, "Sophocles, how are you in sex? Can you still have intercourse with a woman?" "Silence, man," he said. "Most joyfully did I escape it, as though I had run away from a sort of frenzied and savage master." I thought at the time that he had spoken well. (329c)

---

1. In fact, Eros might be suggested by the first image of the torch race. See Dover 1989, 42–45, on the meaning of the word.

For Cephalus and Sophocles, Eros is a "savage master" that drives men mad. This is a description echoed much later in book 9 when Socrates, making explicit for the first time a theme implicitly at work throughout the *Republic*, says, "Eros has from old been called a tyrant" (573b6). Old age, according to Cephalus, is not unwelcome, for it brings "peace and freedom" (329c) from the burning fires of desire.

Eros can drive us crazy. Such, at least is the characterization of it offered by Hesiod and, as mentioned in the third section of chapter 1, explicitly purged from Kallipolean mythology. Recall the first story Socrates censors: Uranus and Cronos as told in Hesiod's *Theogony*. Socrates focuses on only one aspect of the tale, the intergenerational conflict it expresses, but the story is located in a much wider and thoroughly erotic context. Uranus (sky) couples with Gaia (earth) but does not let their offspring "come up to the light" (*Theogony* 156); he keeps them submerged in the earth, causing their mother great pain. Cronos, an earlier son, allies with Gaia. He castrates his father, and the drops of blood that fall into the sea give foamy rise to Aphrodite, the goddess of beautiful love (195). For Hesiod, then, sex and violence, blood and beauty, love and hate, interpenetrate. Eros is, as he says, the "limb-loosener, who conquers the mind and sensible thought in the breasts of all gods and all men" (121–22).

Socrates expunges this version of Eros from Kallipolis. He does so for political reasons: namely, to establish his twin goals of stability and unity. Notably, in discussing Hesiod's stories, he says, "Not even if they were true would I suppose they should be easily told to thoughtless young things" (378a). With this, Plato may invite the reader to wonder whether the Hesiodic account of Eros, however dangerous, could well have some truth to it. Cephalus's remarks about Sophocles thus foreshadow the pattern of erotic repression intrinsic to the foundation of Kallipolis, where it is illegal even to imitate those caught in the throes of Eros (395e.)

In response to Socrates' question, Cephalus explains that if a man is "balanced and good-tempered" (329a), aging is no burden. Socrates, surely not the best of guests, pushes the old man by asking, "Isn't it really because you have lots of money that you find old age untroubling?" (329e). Cephalus agrees but only in part. Because someone with money can pay back all his debts and make sure he has not "done anything unjust to anyone" (330e), he can face the prospect of "having to depart for that other place" (331b) without anxiety or the fear of punishment; however, this applies only to a wealthy man with a good character, for a bad man will no doubt commit unjust acts. Such a malefactor pays a great price even in this life: "The man who finds many unjust deeds in his life often even wakes from his sleep in a fright as children do, and lives in anticipation of evil." By contrast, "to the man who is conscious in himself of no unjust deed, sweet and good hope is ever beside him" (330e).

There is a consistent pattern in Cephalus's behavior and his statements. He values ease. He is glad to be done with erotic madness, happy to be free from the anxiety of debt and the need to lie. He wants to be among the *eukoloi* (329d4), the easygoing (but literally, "those who have good digestion"). He wants to sleep well at night.

Socrates then does something surprising. From the old man's casual remarks he abruptly extracts a definition: "Then isn't this the definition of justice, speaking the truth and giving back what one takes" (331d). Cephalus must be stunned. Surely he had no intention of offering a definition of justice, of seriously grappling with the famous Socratic question, "What is it?" Pursuing this question is strenuous, discomforting, and possibly even counterintuitive. Cephalus is at best an ordinary man: he's glad he's rich and confident he's on the straight and narrow path of virtue; he pays his debts and offers sacrifies to the gods; he doesn't lie, doesn't cheat, he doesn't think. Consequently, as soon as he finds an opportunity to do so, he leaves the house. Turning the conversation over to his son, Polemarchus, "he laughed. And with that he went away to the sacrifices" (331d). Cephalus is a cheerful, conventionally pious man who has good digestion. He is free from the mad disturbance of tyrannical Eros.

Cephalus's departure signals that although it may be a "savage master," Eros is required in order to fuel the pursuit of Socrates' "what-is-it" question. As his interlocutors find out, often to their chagrin, this question forces them to resist their urge to cite particular cases and to strive instead for a level of universality immune to all counterexample.[2] It demands a willingess to leave the familiar and the conventional behind. All this, in turn, requires great effort and, hence, great desire from the interlocutor.

A passage from the *Theaetetus* will help explain. Socrates is conversing with the young Theaetetus. The boy tells him that he studies geometry, astronomy, harmony, and arithmetic (the very subjects

---

2. See "Confusing Universals and Particulars in Plato's Early Dialogues" in Nehamas 1999.

constituting the curriculum articulated in *Republic* 7) with his teacher Theodorus (145c–d). In a manner similar to the way he responded to Cephalus, Socrates asks Theaetetus to extract from this list of particular subjects a definition of knowledge itself, one applicable to all of them.

> It is this very thing about which I am now in perplexity and am not able to grasp sufficiently by myself: what knowledge actually is. Are we able to articulate it? What do you say? (145e)

The bluntness of the unexpected question stuns both Theaetetus and Theodorus into silence. Neither is willing to venture an answer. So Socrates says,

> Why are you silent? Not, Theodorus, because I have been crude [*agroikizomai*] on account of my love of logos and my eagerness [*prothumoumenos*] to have us converse [*dialegesthai*] and come to be friends and interlocutors with one another? (146a)

Notice that Socrates does not say that the "what-is-it" question can be answered, or that if it could, the answer would carry a unique theoretical benefit. Instead, he explains his asking of the question as an expression of his love for *logos*, his spirited pursuit of conversation (*dialegesthai*), and his desire to have friends. In other words, he justifies his question in psychological and practical terms: it gives voice to a deep desire and in turn helps to generate a community of similarly driven inquirers, of friends linked by a passion for a certain sort of conversation. Notice also the word that Socrates uses to describe his asking of the question, which I translate as "crude." It is *agroikizomai*, from the same root as the word used in the phrase in the *Republic* to describe Eros, which Bloom translates as "savage master" (*agrion despotēn*: 329c4). Both derive from *agros*, "field" or "country": that is, what is outside the confines of urban sophistication.

Eros drives us mad and threatens to break loose the bounds of convention (see 572b). The "what-is-it" question is crude, wild, blunt in asking the interlocutor to leave the familiar and easy examples ready at hand and to aim for the universal lying far beyond the conventional. It takes a unique kind of energy to pursue answers to such a question, one similar to that required in the moment of turning around on the divided line, where the philosopher resists the great pull of intellectual gravity and instead of moving from B to C—that is, engaging in technical thinking and generating conventional benefits from the use of applied mathematics—reverses course and heads far upward to the unknown region of the Forms.

When finally persuaded by Socrates to make a stab at answering the question "What is knowledge itself?" young Theaetetus, a wonderful student of mathematics, offers an unsurprising list of examples: geometry, cobblery, and the rest of the *technai* (146d1). Socrates' task in this dialogue is to turn the boy away from reliance on such easy answers and toward the project encapsulated in the "what-is-it" question, to push him into *dialegesthai*, to turn him into a philosophical friend who shares the love of a spirited form of *logos*.

There is a clear parallel between Cephalus and Theodorus. The latter claims to be too old for a question as demanding as "What is knowledge?" He is, he says, "unused to such conversation" (*dialektou*: 146b3). It is left to the younger man, to Theaetetus, to join the hunt. Similarly, when Cephalus bows out in book 1 of the *Republic*, the young and aggressive Polemarchus is eager to give "What is justice?" a shot. So too are Thrasymachus, Glaucon, and Adeimantus. To attempt to answer the question is to strive for unity and universality: that is, to turn around from the particulars and toward the universal. This attempt must be fueled by Eros.

To summarize this line of thought: well before the construction of Kallipolis, the *Republic* begins with the question of Eros. Cephalus, foreshadowing the basic pattern of the legislation offered in books 2–4, welcomes its suppression. He lacks the erotic energy to pursue a Socratic dialogue. By contrast, his aggressive son has it, and so the dialogue can commence. The lesson to be gleaned is clear: without Eros there would be no philosophy. This should hardly be surprising. After all, "philosophy" means "love of wisdom." (See Hyland 1968 for a discussion of this issue.) Since Kallipolis itself is born from the activity of philosophical inquiry into the question of justice, without Eros there would be no Kallipolis. In Kallipolis, however, Eros is counted as a disruptive, subversive force, a potential tyrant, and therefore is systematically suppressed. Eros gives birth to Kallipolis, which in turn attempts to extinguish it.

Eros insinuates itself into the *Republic* in a second way: via the person of Glaucon, clearly the principal interlocutor throughout the dialogue. For example, it is he (and pointedly not Socrates) who agrees to stay in the Piraeus to talk with Polemarchus and company (328b3). He "antes up" for Socrates (337d) and "restores" Thrasymachus's argument, thereby forcing Socrates to continue the discussion after book 1 (357a). Glaucon pushes Socrates toward uttering the noble lie (414d). He does not permit Socrates to delay the task of identifying justice in book 4 (427d). He becomes a "partner in the vote" (450a) and at the outset of book 5 demands that Socrates return to the issue of women and children. He proposes that those guardians who are on campaign be permitted to kiss anyone they happen to love, "either male or female" (468c). He insists that Socrates not duck the question of whether the just city is possible or not: that is, whether Eros can in fact be communalized (471c). He draws a critical distinction between erotic and geometric necessity (458d), and with this demand he forces the conversation to ascend to its philosophical heights. Glaucon insists that the philosopher be distinguished from the lover of sights (475d) and, after forcefully taking over for Adeimantus at a critical juncture in book 6, prohibits Socrates from evading the discussion of the idea of the good (506d4). Glaucon experiences the philosophical feeling of wonder (608d5), and so he raises what may be *the* decisive objection against Kallipolis: namely, the injustice of forcing the philosopher back to the cave in order to govern the prisoners (519d).

In sum, and just as Socrates suggests at 474a, Glaucon is responsible for the forward momentum of the *Republic*. His energy, his passion for the conversation, his forcefulness, and his crucial insights are necessary goads for an otherwise reluctant Socrates. Glaucon is courageous (357a), ready to laugh (398c7), musical (398e1), and spirited (548d8).[3] Most important, he is erotic (474d); he has both a lover (368a) and a beloved (402e). It is thus not surprising when he questions the possibility as well as the desirability of communalizing women and children—that is, of controlling sex (457e1). (See Bloom 1968, 407–8; here Bloom follows Strauss 1978.)

This last point testifies to more than Glaucon's character; it shows his insightfulness, for the failure to control sexual relations is precisely what ruins the putatively just city and brings into being the timocracy (discussed in chapter 3). Indeed, Glaucon becomes even more impressive when he distinguishes between erotic and geometric necessity (458d5), for this distinction diagnoses perfectly the

---

3. As suggested at 536c, spirit, like Eros, is crucial to philosophy. Socrates, e.g., has it: see 497e5 and 506d7.

guardians' failure: they cannot calculate the exact "marriage number" needed to regulate, with technical precision, sexual intercourse in the city. Despite the famous obscurity of its details, the passage makes this much clear: the supposedly wise rulers of the city in speech fail to establish an effective mathematical eugenics. Mathematical *technē* is no match for the erotic necessity animating, and occasionally driving mad, the citizens of Kallipolis. Glaucon properly understands Eros as a tyrant who cannot be completely subdued.

One way of encapsulating the great limitation, the one-sidedness, of Kallipolis is simply to say that Glaucon himself would not be allowed to be one of its citizens. At the same time, however, he is primarily responsible for its coming into being.

2. THE THREE WAVES

Books 2–4 represent the first stage or wave of the *Republic*. With their systematic reform of education, they lay the political foundation for the construction of Kallipolis. Their culmination comes when Socrates announces that "your city would now be founded" (427c6; note, by the way, the pronoun [*soi*] he chooses: he does not say "our city"). He then offers a definition of justice, which he next transfers from city to soul. At that point, the end of book 4, Socrates thinks his job is done, and he is ready to move to the subsequent stage of the argument: the four regimes and corresponding soul types representing the various forms of vice. He is ready, in other words, to move directly to what is actually book 8.

Obviously, however, books 5–7 intervene. Socrates cannot progress as he plans because Polemarchus, the aggressive and erotic son of Cephalus, does not allow him to. He whispers something to Adeimantus, and then the two of them challenge Socrates. "In our opinion," Adeimantus says, "you're taking it easy and robbing us of a whole section of the argument" (449c). Socrates, in elaborating the noble lie, has proposed the elimination of all private sexual relations and the consequent destruction of the family. He has treated this monumentally radical proposal as if it were on a par with, say, a change in parking regulations. Apparently experiencing a delayed reaction, Polemarchus "arrests" (450a) Socrates and demands that he explain further. Books 5–7, then, constitute Socrates' return of a "whole section" (*eidos holon*: 449c2) of the *Republic*. They are a revision of books 2–4, generated by the interruption of Eros.

Socrates reluctantly agrees to elaborate. As I did in the prologue, I cite his crucial caveat:

> How much *logos* you've set in motion, from the beginning again, as it were. . . . You don't know how great a swarm of arguments you're stirring up with what you are now summoning to the bar. I saw it then and passed by so as not to cause a lot of trouble. (450a)

These comments should be puzzling. Why would a return to the theme of sexual regulation require a comprehensive revision of the entire first stage of the *Republic*? Why is Eros so important? Why does it cause so much trouble? Recall that "trouble" (*ochlon*) has political connotations because it can be rendered as "mob, mass, or multitude." When the faction of Adeimantus, Polemarchus, and Glaucon arrest Socrates and force him to discuss further the community of women and children, they are introducing a mass of unpredictable and complex arguments (constituting, of course, the central books of the dialogue).

Eros disturbs, brings trouble, forces us to revise our preconceptions. It destabilizes. Socrates understood this and tried to engage in a Cephalus-like suppression by passing Eros by. The young men would not let him go. And so, here at the quintessentially dialectical moment of the dialogue, the *logos* begins to swell.

In order to reconsider the "community of children and women," Socrates must rethink the very possibility as well as the desirability of Kallipolis itself (450c). This is the sense in which, as he earlier said, the interruption goes to the heart, the *archē* (450a8), of the project. To commence his examination of both the possibility and desirability issues, he uses a metaphor. He must, he says, swim through three waves (457b, 473c), each representing a condition of the possibility of Kallipolis. Furthermore, to swim through a wave means also to determine whether the condition it represents will "be what is best" (450c)—that is, desirable. This traditional Greek metaphor employs the (apparently accurate) notion that waves on the sea come in threes and that the third is the largest, and hence the most difficult through which to swim. Socrates' three waves are these:

(1) "Men and women must share all pursuits in common" (457c). The first condition of the possibility of Kallipolis is equal opportunity. Most important, men and women must both be eligible to become guardians.

(2) "All these women are to belong to all these men in common, and no woman is to live privately with any man. And the children, in their turn, will be in common, and neither will a parent know his own offspring, nor a child his parent" (457d). This is the communalization of Eros, the destruction of the private family.

(3) "Philosophers rule as kings" (473c).

Before confronting the immediate question the three waves present—namely, what in the world is the relationship between the first two and the third?—recall that the Greek for "wave," *kuma*, comes from the verb "to swell" (*kuō*); it can thus name anything that swells. Specifically, it can be translated as "fetus," the swelling of the pregnant woman. Plato clearly targets the word's dual meaning. This digression is, after all, triggered when Eros penetrates the discussion. It is vital to keep this simple point in mind: the famous central books of the *Republic* are a result of Polemarchus's erotic intervention.

The first wave: men and women should have equal access to the top jobs in the city. From a political perspective, Socrates argues, gender is an accidental rather than an essential attribute. Whether a person is male or female is as irrelevant in determining political status as whether that person is bald or long-haired (454c). One's nature—a word repeated several times in this section, (e.g., 453a1, 453b5, 453b8, 453c1)—is determined only by what one learns (455b). Since there is no reason to think that women learn any differently from men, and since ruling is a matter of knowledge rather than physical strength, "there is no practice of a city's governors which belongs to woman because she's woman, or to man because he's man" (455d). Consequently, "the way things are nowadays" in the contemporary world of Athens "proves to be . . . against nature" (456b).[4]

Socrates has successfully navigated the first wave, and the first condition for the possibility of the city has been met. Furthermore, it is also easy to determine that the first wave is beneficial and desirable; it is "for the best." Allowing women to enter into all the same occupations as men brings a higher number of intellectually qualified people into positions of power and importance (456e).

The second wave is far more difficult to accept. "When you see the next [second] one," Socrates warns Glaucon, "you'll say [the first

4. See Keuls 1985 for just how misogynist Athens could be. For an excellent counterpoint, see Saxonhouse and Vlastos in Kraut 1997.

wave] is not so big" (457c). "All these women are to belong to all these men in common, and no woman is to live privately with any man." Furthermore, "children . . . will be in common" (457d). Private sexual alliances are abolished and replaced by politically controlled, tightly regulated relationships. The family disappears, and the city takes responsibility for raising the children.

Socrates seems to treat the benefits of this proposal as self-evident. "As to whether it is beneficial, at least, I don't suppose it would be disputed that the community of women and the community of children are, if possible, the greatest good" (457d). His readiness in saying this is hardly surprising. After all, the primary objectives of his Kallipolis are unity, stability, and a city free from faction. The elimination of the private world and the family might seem a plausible means to achieving these ends. Glaucon, however, has doubts: "There could," he says, "very well be dispute" (457e) about both the benefit and the possibility of the second wave.

Socrates describes Glaucon's worry as a "conspiracy of arguments" (457e2). Nevertheless, he grants the point: thoroughly eliminating the private, erotic realm is problematic. Therefore, and because examining the issue would be so laborious, he advises his friends to postpone this side of the discussion. "I desire," Socrates says, "to put off and consider later in what way it is possible" (458b); for the moment, he simply assumes that it is. Once this assumption is in place, he turns to the desirability question. He begins by offering an analogy between citizens, hunting dogs, and cocks (459a). Just as animals are selectively bred by their owners in order to generate the consistently best offspring, so too in Kallipolis "there is a need for the best men to have intercourse as often as possible with the best women" (459d). To this end, the rulers will begin the practice of eugenics. They will, for example, "take the offspring of the good, and bring them into the pen to certain nurses who live apart in a certain section of the city. And those of the worse . . . they will hide away in an unspeakable and unseen place" (460c). The key objective is to ensure that "the guardians' species is going to remain pure" (460c).

Just like the noble lie, the eugenics program that Socrates suggests here in book 5 foreshadows the "marriage number" of book 8 in being disinctly arithmetical in character: "The number of the marriages we'll leave to the rulers in order that they may most nearly preserve the same number of men" (460a). The goal of Socrates' proposal is to keep the population at a numerical constant. (In this regard it harks back to the city of pigs, in which the citizens "have sweet intercourse with one another, and [do] not produce children beyond their means": 372b.) Other strictures on Eros are similarly arithmetic. For example, women and men are each given a distinct number of years in which they will be allowed to procreate: the former from age twenty to forty, the latter from age twenty-five to fifty-five.

A clear risk the city faces is that because biological parents do not know their offspring, there will be incest. Again, Socrates proposes an arithmetical solution: "All the children born in the tenth month, and in the seventh, from the day a man becomes a bridegroom, he will call the males sons and the females daughters" (461d). As commentators since Aristotle (*Politics* 2.1) have noticed, this is not a very effective deterrent against incest. What is most striking about it here is not its efficacy but its arithmetical character.

Ultimately, Socrates relies on the criterion of unity to argue for the benefit of his politicization of Eros. Since there is no "greater evil for a city than what splits it and makes it many instead of one," and since "the privacy of such things [erotic relations]" (462b) threatens its unity, the second wave is counted as beneficial. The "community of women and children" generates "a community of pleasures and pains" among the guardians" of Kallipolis (464a). Hence, it has "turned out to be the cause of the greatest good to our city" (464b).

At 466d, Socrates finally seems ready to return to the possibility question. Instead of actually doing so, however, he engages in a long (466d–471c) digression about military matters. Eventually, Glaucon becomes impatient: "But, Socrates, I think that if one were to allow you to speak about this sort of thing, you would never remember what you previously set aside in order to say all this. Is it possible for this regime to come into being, and how is it ever possible?" (471c).

Socrates confesses to ducking the question. Indeed, he never specifically discusses exactly how to regulate sexual relationships in Kallipolis (until, of course, he comes to book 8 and the marriage number, where he explains the Kallipolean failure to achieve a mathematically based eugenics). What he does say, however, suggests why he ducks it. He proposes, for example, that "certain subtle lots must be fabricated so that the ordinary man will blame chance rather than the rulers for each union" (460a). He thus acknowledges the ordinary human impulse to resist losing the privacy of sexual relations and the family. In other words, human Eros will make it remarkably difficult to swim through the second wave. As if to anticipate his inability to address it, Socrates goes so far as to diminish the importance of the possibility question. A painter "who draws a pattern of what the fairest human being would be like . . . but can't prove that it's also possible that such a man come into being" (472d) is not to be counted as inferior.

Even if he manages to avoid the question of sex, Socrates must eventually, because of Glaucon's insistence, tackle the possibility question. To do so, he dives directly into the third wave: "Unless philosophers rule as kings or those now called kings and chiefs genuinely and adequately philosophize, and political power and philosophy coincide in the same place . . . there is no rest from ills for the cities" (473d).

This is strange: discussion of the third wave takes the place of an argument on behalf of the possibility of the second (471c–e). The central books of the *Republic*, famed for their excursions into metaphysics and epistemology, are generated as a result of Socrates' need to explicate the political regulation of sex.

In order for the metaphor to retain its integrity, the second and third waves must be intimately related. Thus, there must be a strong connection between Eros and philosophy. But what is it? Simply this: philosophy, as its etymology suggests, is an erotic activity. (Rosen 1988 is excellent on this matter.) Socrates makes this point very clear when he takes up the challenge presented to him by Glaucon. After hearing the particulars of the third wave, Glaucon is aghast:

> What a phrase and argument you have let burst out. Now that it's said, you can believe that very many men, and not ordinary ones, will on the spot throw off their clothes, and stripped for action, taking hold of whatever weapon falls under the hand of each, run full speed at you to do wonderful deeds. If you don't defend yourself with speech and get away, you'll really pay the penalty in scorn. (474a)

An extraordinary image: naked men ready for battle attacking a Socrates who has had the temerity to propose that philosophers should rule. To respond to the furious incredulity of these men, Socrates must "distinguish for them whom we mean when we dare to assert the philosophers must rule" (474b). This is important: the long digression Socrates is about to take into the central books of the *Republic* begins with his need to explain *to the naked men attacking him* who the philosopher is. And to do this, he immediately turns to Eros: "Do you remember," he asks Glaucon, "that when we say a man loves [*philein*] something, it is rightly said of him, he must . . . cherish all of it?" (474c).[5] *Distinguishing* the philosopher means explaining the nature of his or her desires. Thus Socrates soon says that a philosopher is a "desirer of wisdom" (475b8), a "lover of the sight of truth" (475e4). Most strikingly, he describes philosophical natures as "always in love with (*erōsin*) that learning which discloses to them something of the being that is always and does not wander about, driven by generation and decay" (485b).

Socrates also says this:

It is the nature of the real lover of learning [*philomathēs*] to strive for what is; and he does not tarry by each of the many things opined to be but goes forward and does not lose the keenness of his passionate love [*erōtos*] nor cease from it before he grasps the nature itself of each thing which is with the part of the soul fit to grasp a thing of that sort; and it is the part akin to it that is fit. And once near it and coupled with what really is, having begotten intelligence and truth, he knows and lives truly, is nourished and so ceases from his labor pains, but not before. (490b)

These passages (cf. 499c1–2) are critical. First, they powerfully revise and enrich the tripartite psychology of book 4. There reason was reduced to calculation and radically separated from desire. There the "love of learning" (435e7) was mentioned but could not be fully accounted for. Here reason has expanded and has itself become animated by Eros. A lover of learning strives for being not with a part of the soul but with "the soul as a whole." Second, with their bold use of erotic language, these passages form the prelude to the topic typically thought to be quintessentially Platonic, the "theory of ideas." Even if book 6, with its Idea of the Good and the divided line, seems to disclose the heart of Platonic metaphysics, these famous images are embedded in Socrates' *psychological* portrait of the philosopher. The Idea of the Good and the divided line do not continue the project of articulating the structure of being as being. Instead, they help Socrates delineate ("for them") the philosopher's erotic soul.

To reformulate: Socrates' discussion of philosophy has two sides,

5. This passage seems to imply that Eros clouds one's judgment. A wine lover does not typically love *all* wines, even bad ones.

the subjective and the objective. The former describes the erotic nature of the philosophical soul; the latter, what it loves—namely, "the
being that is always" (485b2). The two sides are not independent of
each other. "Being that is always" becomes visible in the *Republic*
not simply as being but only as the object of the philosopher's desire.
It comes into view only because of the erotic striving to delight in and
articulate it (see 476b). In a parallel fashion, it is impossible to talk
about the soul of the philosopher without discussing the ultimate object of his or her desire: that is, what "is always." In hot pursuit of the
"what-is-it" question, it strives for stability. This does not imply that
the philosophical soul is stable. In fact, quite the opposite: driven by
the "savage master" Eros, philosophers love and seek madly to obtain, to move forcefully toward, what is distinctly other than themselves and far beyond human reach.[6] To re-invoke a metaphor from
chapter 1, a philosophical soul—explicated as it is by the "hydraulic
model of desire" at 485d—is fluid even as it seeks to become dry.

To elaborate: consider Socrates' remarks as he attempts to explain,
to Glaucon and the naked men attacking him, who the philosopher
is. The one "who is willing to taste every kind of learning with gusto,
and who approaches learning with delight, and is insatiable, we shall
justly assert to be a philosopher" (475c). Glaucon wonders whether
this description isn't too broad. Wouldn't it cover all sorts of
"strange" (475d1) people, lovers of sights and of sounds who delight
in their senses? Socrates acknowledges that such people are indeed
"like philosophers." After all, both types of human beings are lovers.
But philosophers are "lovers of the sight of the truth," not of particular items. To explain what he means, he broaches his notion of the
Forms.

The beautiful, Socrates says, is the opposite of the ugly.[7] Since they
are opposites, "they are two." Each, however, is "also one." In other
words, each can be counted as a unit. The same reasoning applies to
justice and injustice, good and bad, and "all the forms; each is itself
one, but by showing themselves everywhere in a community with ac-
tions, bodies, and one another, each looks like [*phainesthai*] many"
(476a).

With these remarks, Socrates might seem poised to present a
metaphysical argument. But note how he subtly changes the subject:

6. This statement is a version of Diotima's point (in the *Symposium*) that we love
what we lack, or Socrates' (in the *Phaedo*) that philosophy is the preparation for death.
7. Bloom always uses "fine" to translate *kalon*. His motivation is clear and reasonable, but for the sake of familiarity I opt for "beautiful."

"Well now," he says to Glaucon, "this is how I separate them" (*tautē . . . diairō*: 476a9). Bloom's translation is slightly inaccurate: in the Greek there is no "them." Literally, the phrase is just "in this way I separate." Separate what? Even with his importation of "them," Bloom retains the necessary ambiguity. "Separate" initially seems to refer to the distinction Socrates has just drawn between particulars and Forms. But Socrates is looking forward, not back. He does not separate particulars from forms, the one from the many, but "the lovers of sights, the lovers of arts, and the practical men" from the "philosophers" (476a). His distinction is psychological, not metaphysical.

> The lovers of hearing and the lovers of sights, on the one hand . . . surely delight in fair sounds and colors and shapes and all that craft makes from such things, but their thought [*dianoia*] is unable to see and delight in the nature of the beautiful itself. (476b)

Lovers of sights, "unable to see" the beautiful itself, do not suffer merely a cognitive deficiency, not simply a failure to comprehend the implications of a metaphysical argument about particulars and Forms. Equally if not more important is their incapacity to "delight" in Forms. They are psychologically resistant to the attractions of "things themselves."

> That good man who doesn't believe that there is anything beautiful in itself and an idea of the beautiful itself, which always stays the same in all respects, but does hold that there are many beautiful things, this lover of sights . . . can in no way endure it if anyone asserts the beautiful is one. (479a)

Not only are lovers of sight indifferent to the beautiful itself; they actively resist someone who even suggests that human beings might have access to, and therefore should pursue, this sort of intelligible structure. Indeed, it makes them angry. For them—and a good instance of "them" is of course the Sophists—reality is particularized, and they like it that way. This is a psychological disposition, not a philosophical position. Beauty itself just leaves them cold. They warm instead to the multiplicitous dance of particulars in the world around them. In this sense, they can take Wittgenstein, who complains about Socrates' "contemptuous attitude towards the particular case" (1965, 18), as their champion.

(There are other instances of this sort of extreme and almost bizarre anger generated by even the mere mention of intelligible "things themselves." One is the anger of those "disbelievers" who, Socrates claims, have forced him to forget he was playing and to speak too seriously (see 536c). Another is found in the sailors on the "ship of state" who, upon hearing the proposition that virtue is teachable, "are ready to cut to pieces the man who says it is" (488b). While it is easy to see why these non-philosophers might object, it is difficult to understand why they would resort to mutilation.)

Next comes a passage (476e–480a) frequently commented on by philosophers on the hunt for Platonic epistemology. As Fine puts it, this is "Plato's only lengthy attempt to distinguish knowledge from belief" (1978, 122). She argues against the common view that Plato distinguishes the two by means of their objects, with knowledge being only of Forms, and belief only of sensibles. This view commits Plato to what is often described as the "two worlds theory" (122). For Fine, by contrast, "knowledge and belief are distinguished, not by their different sets of objects, but by their truth implications. Knowledge, but not belief, entails truth. . . . Plato has precluded neither knowledge of the sensible nor beliefs about Forms" (139). On the basis of this argument, Fine gladly gives up the "two worlds theory."

Fine's work, like that of her opponents, overlooks what is conspicuous on the surface of this passage: *Socrates is not engaged in epistemology or metaphysics*. Instead, he is trying to explain to Glaucon, and the naked men attacking him, the difference between two types of human beings. Philosophers are peculiarly disposed to long for being and so turn away from the particulars. By contrast, lovers of sights are delighted by particularity as such and experience a strong resistance to thinking the world to be otherwise.

Both sides of this story, the subjective and the objective, are prominent when Socrates discusses the Idea of the Good. It is first articulated in psychological terms:

> Isn't it clear that many men would choose to do, possess, and enjoy the reputation for things that are opined to be just and fair, even if they aren't, while, when it comes to good things, no one is satisfied with what is opined to be so but each seeks the things that are [ta onta], and from here on out everyone despises the opinion. (505d)

This is neither a metaphysical nor an epistemological claim. If anything, Socrates seems to be reporting the results of some sort of empirical research. Most men, he tells us, are able to enjoy what seems to be just or beautiful (505d), even if it is not. I may know, for example, that cheating on my income taxes violates a law and in this sense is unjust, but I may rationalize the action by arguing to myself that in some other sense it is good to do so. I may thoroughly enjoy the possession of a painting that I like, even if I suspect that it is not really beautiful. In general, it is possible to sustain the enjoyment of appearances (*ta dokounta*: 505d6) of the beautiful or the just. But when it comes to what is good, only what is can satisfy. By definition, the Good must be good. I can enjoy the painting that I suspect is not really beautiful because I think it is good to enjoy it. But I cannot enjoy what only seems to be good if I think it is not or may not be. This is so because there is no higher value to appeal to in order to rationalize the shortcomings of the appearances. Everything else can get by even while falling short, because the deficiency can be remedied by reference to what is good. But the Good allows no such accommodation. If it is deficient, it is unsatisfying. The Good demands being good.[8]

Socrates initially defines the Idea of the Good as

> what every soul pursues and for the sake of which it does everything. The soul divines that it is something but is at a loss about it and unable to get a sufficient grasp of just what it is, or to have a stable trust such as it has about the rest. And because this is so, the soul loses any profit there might been in the rest. (505e)

The Idea of the Good is the ultimate object of desire. Substitutes or appearances are unsatisfying, as ordinary human action testifies: we strive for and then latch on to this or that project or person or city or car or meal or work of art, but these do not completely satisfy. Because they are not entirely good, these objects are soon left behind. The sheer restlessness of human desire continually propels us forward. Most people, Socrates suggests, sense, or have a vague intuition of, something missing from their lives. (Why else would they strive?) But articulation eludes them, for they cannot get a "sufficient grasp" (505e2) of "what it is." They are unable to answer the question "What is the Good?" As a result, they are left without any "stable trust" (505e2–3). They are at a loss, ever in pursuit of they know not what. By contrast, philosophers, mad lovers of what always is, understand the ground of their own restlessness and thus know the right question to ask: "What is the Good itself?"

8. Imitating Socrates, I shift from "Idea of the Good" to "the Good." See Roochnik 1996 for an explanation of why Plato makes this move. Also, see Lachterman 1989 for an excellent discussion of "the good."

Curiously, just as on the subjective side the philosopher is described in erotic terms, so too on the objective side is the Good itself. It has offspring—namely, the sun—which is "begot in a proportion with itself" (508b13). The Good can do what, as the failure of the marriage number so wonderfully demonstrates, human beings cannot: give birth in "proportion with itself"—that is, in a perfectly mathematical manner. By aiming to have gold-souled people reproduce only with, and then give birth only to, analogously gold-souled people, the rulers of Kallipolis attempt to achieve just this sort of proportional birthing. Yet citizens "will at some time beget children when they should not" (546b), and there will be a "chaotic mixing of iron with silver and of bronze with gold" (547a). The Good is thus the ultimate Kallipolean fantasy: it represents the subordination of Eros to *arithmos*.

The basic elements are now in place. Eros is a "savage master" who drives the philosopher to ask the crude "what-is-it" question. Philosophers, for whatever reason, thus reverse the normal direction of human intellectual activity. Instead of going downward to and reveling in particulars, they attempt to defy the force of gravity and fly upward to the universal Form which, if properly articulated, would somehow supply the answer to their question. Philosophers, impressed as they are by the passage of time, which renders fleeting the possession of all things, seek to grasp securely in *logos* what is ultimately stable: the Idea of the Good. The Platonic dialogues express both sides of this story: the motion of Eros and the stability of the Good. As argued in chapter 1, *arithmos* is the crucial intermediary. The lowly business of the one, two, and three intrudes into, and then invites and inspires us to move beyond, the "barbaric bog" of ordinary life.

Kallipolis, with its tripartite class system and the psychology it generates, represents an excessively arithmetical regime. It represses Eros and is too rigid, too dominated by the dictates of calculation. It is negated by the interruption of Eros at the beginning of book 5. As a result, the second wave of the dialogue is erotically charged from the outset, and books 5–7 significantly advance beyond the limitations of books 2–4. Most important, with the introduction of Eros, philosophy enters the *Republic,* and the long march to the central images of the sun, the divided line, and the cave can begin. Nonetheless, the second wave of the dialogue is also limited: it takes place within the confines of Kallipolis. As a result (and as the next section demonstrates), the erotic life of the philosopher is precarious, perhaps even impossible.

With the failure of the marriage number in book 8, Eros finally overtakes Kallipolis, and the tightly wound regime comes apart at the seams. Eros in its tyrannical and polymorphous manifestations fully unfolds in books 8–10. A regime far different from Kallipolis is required to accommodate it. Kallipolis, then, does not represent Plato's political or theoretical ideal. Instead, it is a moment in the dialectical development of the *Republic* as a whole.

3. KALLIPOLIS VERSUS THE *REPUBLIC*

I want to bring into sharper focus the crucial distinction between Kallipolis, understood as a moment (i.e., the city Socrates constructs in books 2–7), and the *Republic* in its entirety. With the failure of the marriage number, Kallipolis falls apart. It does so because it stands at odds with the very conditions that gave rise to it. The dialogue as a whole, principally composed of the conversation between Socrates and Glaucon, is erotically charged. Kallipolis, by stark contrast, suppresses Eros at every turn. There is thus a basic tension between the city generated by the speakers and the speakers themselves. Simply put, if Kallipolis were to come into being, then the *Republic* could not. But since Kallipolis requires the *Republic* in order to come into being, it contains in itself the seeds of its dissolution.[9]

To put this argument into abstract form, let K stand for "Kallipolis comes into being," and R for "the *Republic* is allowed to take place." My thesis is this: if K $\rightarrow$ –R; if –R $\rightarrow$ –K; $\therefore$ if K $\rightarrow$ –K; $\therefore$ –K. In other words, Kallipolis undermines itself. As I explain more fully in chapter 3, however, when comprehended via a dialectical reading of the *Republic*, this undermining—this essential tension between the abstract ideal of Kallipolis and the human urges giving birth to it—is itself enormously instructive.

A final formuation of the thesis: Kallipolis requires philosophers to become rulers. But as the tripartite psychology itself suggests, Socrates' city in speech cannot in fact sustain the development of philosophers, for the reasons just presented in the preceding section: philosophy is essentially erotic, and this erotic energy would be choked by the tight regulations of books 2–4. Furthermore, as chapter 3 argues, the exclusively mathematical curriculum proposed for the

9. For somewhat similar arguments, see Clay 1988 and Hyland 1989 and 1995.

guardians in book 7 (arithmetic, plane geometry, solid geometry, theoretical astronomy, and harmonics) is too one-sided to nourish the philosophical soul. As Socrates makes clear in books 8–10, a life of freedom and an exposure to human diversity is needed for that.

To elaborate the sense in which Kallipolis and the *Republic* as a whole stand in tension (if K → –R), consider these eight examples.

(1) The simplest: in Kallipolis, the guardians will not have private homes (416d, 543b). The *Republic* itself, however, takes place in the private home of Cephalus. In this straightforward but perhaps not trivial sense, the *Republic* could not occur in Kallipolis.

(2) A more significant example: in book 3, Socrates makes the following proposal concerning the censorship of poetry:

> Because I suppose we'll say that what both poets and prose writers say concerning the most important things about human beings is bad—that many happy men are unjust, and many wretched ones just, and that doing injustice is profitable if one gets away with it, but justice is someone else's good and one's own loss. We'll forbid them to say such things. (392a–b)

In Kallipolis it is forbidden to describe just men as wretched and injustice as profitable. Presumably, making such statements would badly influence those citizens who listen to (or read) them. But the entire project of books 2–7 is generated as a response to Glaucon's saying precisely such things at 358b–362b. In an elaborate "thought experiment," he tells a version of the ring of Gyges story (359d–360a) in which perfect injustice is perfectly profitable. He sketches a scenario in which the just man would be saddled with a reputation for total injustice and duly suffer the consequences. Glaucon seems almost inspired as he paints the picture. The just man, he says, will be "whipped; he'll be racked; he'll be bound; he'll have both his eyes burned out; and, at the end, when he has undergone every sort of evil, he'll be crucified" (361e3–362a2).

Glaucon's lengthy speech, then, explicitly violates the strictures placed on poetry in Kallipolis. So too do the remarks of Adeimantus, which follow immediately upon Glaucon's tale. (Note in particular Adeimantus's quotation of Hesiod at 364d, a passage that no doubt would be censored in Kallipolis.) In fact, Socrates himself, when he begins to interrogate old Cephalus (328e), cites a line from the *Iliad* which, since it is spoken by Priam and alludes to the wretchedness of death, would violate the Kallipolean ban on all poems that "disparage Hades' domain" (368d).

If Glaucon's tale of Gyges were to be expurgated, however, *there would be no reason to construct Kallipolis*, for it is this story that forces Socrates to continue the argument he began with Thrasymachus. It plunges him into his extraordinary investigation of the question of whether justice is a good to be valued "both for itself and for what comes out of it" (358a3). Without Glaucon's forceful intervention, Socrates would have been "freed from the argument" (357a1) and could presumably have continued on his way up from the Piraeus and back home to Athens.

Glaucon's explicit violation of a Kallipolean law discloses a basic pattern. To generate his massive argument concerning justice, Socrates needs to be intensely challenged by a "courageous" (357a3) interlocutor such as Glaucon. (This is a challenge Socrates manifestly welcomes: see 367e.) Political philosophy, it seems, is born from such questioning. Just such questioning would, however, be stifled in Kallipolis.

(3) In Kallipolis, the study of philosophy is not begun until the age of thirty (537d).[10] If, as many commentators think, the dramatic date of the *Republic* is 411, and if Glaucon and Adeimantus, who were Plato's brothers, were reasonably close in age to Plato (born 427), they would not have been permitted to engage in philosophical discussion. But of course they do. The *Republic*'s youthful spirit would not be allowed free expression in Kallipolis.[11]

(4) Consider next the regulation of imitative and narrative poetry (395b–397d). It is highly restrictive, allowing only "unmixed imitation of the decent man" (397d5). In book 10 the restriction is even more severe: "Only so much of poetry as is hymns to gods or celebration of good men should be admitted into a city" (607a). (The apparent discrepancy between these two passages is discussed in the third section of chapter 3.) But the *Republic* itself, which is entirely spoken by Socrates, includes imitation not only of decent men (such as, presumably, Socrates himself) but also of the (presumably) indecent (Thrasymachus and Cleitophon) and of those whose characters are uncertain (Polemarchus, Glaucon, Adeimantus). Again, if Kallipolis

---

10. Even then, it is at best a very attenuated form of philosophy that is studied.
11. Furthermore, although men are prohibited from generating children after the age of fifty-five (460e), Socrates, at least according to the *Phaedo*, is well known for having done just this.

were actually to come into being, the *Republic*, on strictly stylistic grounds, would be outlawed.[12]

(5) Kallipolis, the most rigid and monocultural of regimes, sharply curtails "musical" innovation.

> For they [the guardians] must beware of change to a strange [*kainon*] form of music, taking it to be a danger to the whole. For never are the ways of music moved without the great political laws being moved. (424c)

Yet the *Republic* is born from Socrates' desire to go down to the Piraeus, the cosmopolitan seaport, in order to see *new* music: specifically, a religious festival (327a). Furthermore, he is induced to stay there by Adeimantus's announcement that "at sunset there will be a torch race on horseback for the goddess." Socrates seems impressed: "On horseback?" he replies. "That is novel" (*kainon*: 328a3). (For passing the torch as a sexual metaphor, see *Laws* 776b.) The first words of the dialogue, then, show Socrates seeking out novelty, "multiculturalism," and "diversity," all of which would be forbidden in Kallipolis. (Note also the ban on free travel in Kallipolis: 420a.)

(6) The god whose festival Socrates has come to see is Bendis (354a), who is new to the Athenians. Such theological innovation would, of course, be prohibited in Kallipolis, not only by the general ban on innovation but also by the official theology. Gods, in the politically sanctioned myths, do not come to be (381c), yet it seems that for the Athenians, at least, Bendis *did* come to be. Therefore, her arrival could not be conceived of, let alone celebrated, in Kallipolis.

(7) Kallipolis prohibits assaults on and the dishonoring of elders (465a). Yet several critical transitions of the *Republic* are generated by what can be construed (at least metaphorically) as just such assaults. The dialogue begins with Polemarchus forcing the elder Socrates to stay in the Piraeus (327c). Later in book 1, Thrasymachus "flung himself" (336b) at Socrates in order to change the direction the conversation was taking. At the beginning of book 5 (449c–450a), when Adeimantus and Polemarchus (soon joined by Glaucon) force Socrates to return to the topic of the "community of women and children," Socrates describes himself as having been "arrested" (450a5)—a clear intimation, however metaphorical, of assault. Even more explicit is Socrates' response when Glaucon urges him not to

---

12. Actually, the *Republic* is reported in indirect discourse.

tarry but to pursue directly the question of whether the city in speech is possible: "All of a sudden . . . you have, as it were, assaulted my argument, and you have no sympathy for me and my loitering" (472a). Glaucon's "assault" (echoed in even stronger terms at 474a), which would be prohibited in Kallipolis, is needed for the *Republic* to proceed to its treatment of the "philosopher king."

(8) As already discussed, the essential purpose of Kallipolean legislation is to end factionalism. "Have we any greater evil for a city than what splits it and makes it many instead of one?" Socrates asks (462a8–b2). The answer is no (cf. 444b). "That city in which most say 'my own' and 'not my own' about the same thing, and in the same way" (462c) is the best-governed city. The noble lie, introduced in book 3 (414d–e), is specifically designed to inhibit the growth of factions and disseminate a sense of common purpose among the citizens.

Faction, of course, does arise and ultimately causes the breakdown of Kallipolis (see 545d). Moreover, in at least an intellectual sense, it is integral to book 1 of the *Republic*. Socrates and Polemarchus, for example, are a faction united against the relativism of Cleitophon and Thrasymachus (340a–c). When Adeimantus, Polemarchus, and Glaucon arrest Socrates and force him to discuss further the community of women and children, they constitute a faction, as well. (Recall the phrase "conspiracy of arguments" at 457e2.) The point is this: Kallipolis is single-minded in its quest to bring order and end factionalism, but the *Republic*, understood as a dialogue between different kinds of human beings, is bred on factionalism. It is full of the very trouble that Socrates as founder aims to avoid. Such trouble may well be defused (however temporarily) in the defactionalized, sanitized Kallipolis, but doing so would rob the *Republic* of the impetus it requires to construct an ideal city.

To summarize: as foreshadowed by Cephalus's reference to Sophocles, Kallipolis essentially depends on the repression of the erotic energy of both city and soul. Eros, after all, is a "tyrant" (573b6) and must be subdued. If Eros is constrained in Kallipolis by its regulatory fetters, however, then the desire for wisdom, which is consistently described by Socrates in erotic terms, could not be nourished. This result would prove to be devastating. After all, *the* salient feature of Kallipolis is its third wave: the rule of philosophers. As Socrates puts it, "There would always have to be present in the city something possessing the same understanding of the regime as you, the lawgiver, had when you were setting down the laws" (497c).[13] Therefore, should philosophers not be able to rule, the city would be undermined.

In addition to the tripartite psychology—which, by reducing reason to calculation and then separating it from desire, cannot account for the desire to be reasonable—the key expression of this point is found in the allegory of the cave. Socrates does not allow the liberated prisoners who have made it to the upper world and seen the sun to remain aboveground. Instead, he compels (*anangkasai*: 519c9) them to return to the cave and there to participate fully in political affairs. Glaucon forcefully protests: "What? . . . Are we to do them an injustice, and make them live a worse life when a better is possible for them?" (519d). As Eric Brown (2000, 1) points out, "Seven times Socrates or Glaucon invokes some variant of *anangkē* (necessity, compulsion) to account for the philosophers' decision not to rule."[14] This exchange is, to say the least, a hotly contested passage. Indeed, Brown goes so far as to proclaim that "the fate of the *Republic* hangs in its balance" (2000, 2). If an unjust application of force lies at the heart of Kallipolis, then the putatively beautiful city implodes.

The debate has raged, notably in a well-known exchange between Leo Strauss (1978) and Myles Burnyeat(1985). For Strauss, the injustice of making unwilling philosophers rule tokens the failure of the perfectly just city.

> Only the non-philosophers could compel the philosophers to take care of the city. But, given the prejudice against the philosophers, this compulsion will not be forthcoming if the philosophers do not in the first place persuade the non-philosophers to compel the philosophers to rule over them, and this persuasion will not be forthcoming, given the philosophers' unwillingness to rule. We arrive then at the conclusion that the just city is not possible because of the philosophers' unwillingness to rule. (Strauss 1978, 124)

A sizable literature argues against this view (Brown 2000 has a thorough bibliography). Most commentators take their bearings from Socrates' immediate response to Glaucon's objection: "It's not the concern of law that any one class in the city fare exceptionally well,

---

13. This is a crucial way in which Socrates' political story differs from traditional ones: the founder must be present in the city after it is founded.

14. The passages he lists are 500d4, 519e4, 520a8, 520e3, 521b7, 539e3, and 540b5.

but it contrives to bring this about for the whole city" (519e). This passage suggests that the compulsion Socrates applies to the philosophers in the cave is the force of reason and hence anything but unjust. On this reading, an argument persuades the philosopher to fulfill his obligation to serve the city that nurtured him. Consider Burnyeat's rebuttal of Strauss:

> Socrates is in fact arguing that the just city is possible because of the philosophers' unwillingness to rule. Willing rulers want to rule because of something they will get out of it, for themselves or for their country. Not so the philosophers of the ideal city; their complete dedication to the higher world of mathematics and active philosophical discussion guarantees that ruling can give them nothing that they value. In place of the partialities that corrupt the rulers we are familiar with, they will put the requirements of impartial justice. Just so, it is the requirements of impartial justice that persuade them to govern in the first place. Nobody else could be so compelled, but these devotees of pure reason are compelled to rule by the force of the reasoned argument which is put to them—not by the nonphilosophers but by the founding fathers of the city, Socrates and his interlocutors. This argument is that the philosophers owe a debt to the ideal city for providing the liberal education in mathematics and philosophy that teaches them to know and love justice. They will rule for justice's sake and that alone, to requite a debt rather than because they think it is a great good to be in charge of the city. (Burnyeat 1985, 34)

This move is crucial to commentators such as Burnyeat, for they view the *Republic* as an argument whose many parts must, in order to be successful, consistently contribute to the conclusion that philosophers rule the city. For them, disaster would ensue should Glaucon's objection of 519d prove to have merit. By contrast, the arguments I develop throughout this book—some of which are distantly related to those of Strauss, and many of which conclude that there is a fundamental tension between Kallipolis and the erotically driven philosopher who conceives it—suggest that Glaucon may be quite right. It would be an injustice—a violation of the principle that citizens should do only the work that belongs to them—to force the philosopher to return to the thoroughly unphilosophical cave. Furthermore, it would be quite useless. Even before the philosopher returns, Socrates says, there is already "wisdom" (*sophia*: 516c5) in the cave; it belongs to the prisoner who is "sharpest at making out the things [the shadows] that go by, and [who] most remembers which of them are accustomed to pass before, which after, and which at the same time as others, and who is thereby most able to divine what is going to come" (516c). In other words, cave wisdom requires familarity with the sequence of shadows projected on the cave wall by the puppeteers, and the consequent ability to predict future projections. This amounts to something like "practical wisdom": that is, knowledge of how those human puppeteers responsible for casting the shadows are likely to behave. By contrast, the liberated prisoner attains what looks like theoretical wisdom. He beholds the "light of the stars and the moon" (516a) and, finally, the sun, nonhuman objects all. What good would this do in helping to run things down in the dark and smoky regions of the cave?

I thus agree with Strauss rather than Burnyeat on this issue. There are several reasons to think Glaucon's objection at 519d is decisive. It tokens precisely the confict between Kallipolis and the *Republic* elucidated above. Quite simply, despite requiring philosophy in order to come into being, Kallipolis is not itself philosophical, for its essential thrust is to constrain and repress the erotic impulse from which philosophy necessarily originates. As a consequence, the putatively just and beautiful city in speech is, as Strauss puts it, "not possible." He oversimplifies when he says that this is true "because of the philosopher's unwillingess to rule." That is only one reason. There are others, and they are deeper, and the purpose of this chapter has been to articulate them.

In the *Republic*, Kallipolis comes into being and then passes away. An arithmetical or logical or technical "ideal" is postulated and then subjected to dialectical pressure. It must be negated. But this is not to say it is junked. Instead, it is located in its proper context, as a moment in the unfolding of the dialogue. It is reasonable for philosophers to begin their thinking-through of both city and soul in arithmetical terms. Failure to do so would deny a fundamental inflection of human thought: namely, loyalty to the PNO and the possibility of logical, atemporal structure. But it would be equally a failure to exaggerate the role of *arithmos* in human thinking and thus to deny the intrusive role of Eros and its essential relationship to time (i.e., its ever moving toward the future in order to secure the object of desire). The *Republic* does not fail. It denies neither.

A final encapsulation of the argument presented in this section: Kallipolis must fall apart because it suppresses Eros so thoroughly that not only would it undermine its own existence but would stifle all the many blossomings of the human spirit. Not only would philosophy disappear—and for Plato this is of course the fundamental, perhaps even the only real, issue—but so too would privacy, artistic freedom, disagreement, and political debate, all of which have been shown to be essential to the *Republic* itself. Much like numbers, Kallipolis, however beautiful, should therefore not be counted as an ultimate conceptual ideal: that is as a serious model for constructing a city or living a life. Instead, what is needed is a regime that allows the flourishing of Eros. This regime is democracy, where both for better and for worse, the citizens live amid "the liberation and unleashing of unnecessary and useless pleasures" (561a). Kallipolis, with its rigid class system and fierce restraint of speech, action, and Eros, is infamously antidemocratic. And yet, as has been implied by all the examples cited above, the very context from which Kallipolis emerges is democratic. For this reason, then, Plato's *Republic*, far from being the condemnation of democracy it is typically thought to be, is in fact a qualified (and dialectical) supporter of it.

CHAPTER THREE

Democracy, Psychology, Poetry

I. DEMOCRACY

Finally, after the long detour of books 5–7, Socrates returns to the "mistaken" (449a, 554a) regimes and corresponding soul types in book 8. Following the failure of the marriage number and the consequent dissolution of the best regime (i.e., the aristocracy: 544e6), the timocracy or rule by the spirited lovers of victory (545b6), emerges. After this comes the oligarchy, rule by the wealthy few (550c); democracy, initially characterized as rule by the many poor (557a); and finally the tyranny, the regime whose ruler putatively lives 729 times more unpleasantly than do the philosopher-kings of Kallipolis (587e).

The manner in which Socrates narrates this sequence and conceives of the relationship between regime and corresponding individual is crucial to my argument. In this section I concentrate solely on Socrates' description of democracy. In particular, I argue against the widely held view that Plato was the archenemy of democracy (St. Croix 1981, 412). That view, even if wrong, is an immediately plausible response to the *Republic*; after all, Kallipolis is a democrat's nightmare. Still, from this fact alone one cannot legitimately infer that Plato is radically antidemocratic. Kallipolis, after all, is not equivalent to the *Republic* and hence cannot by itself represent Plato's views. Instead, it is a construction project undertaken by the participants in the dialogue, all for the purpose of making "easier" Socrates' task of persuading Glaucon and Adeimantus of the superiority of justice to injustice (368e–369a). Kallipolis is a stage, a moment, in a long conversation that terminates at the beginning of book 8. As argued in the previous chapter, the forces conspiring to cause its dissolution are contained in the very conditions that generate it: that is, in the philosophical dialogue of the *Republic* itself.

The following lines, spoken by Socrates, contain the essential thesis of this section:

Thanks to its license, [democracy] contains all species of regimes, and it is probably necessary for the man who wishes to organize a city, as we were just doing, to go to a city under a democracy. He would choose the sort that pleases him, like a man going into a general store of regimes, and, once having chosen, he would thus establish his regime (557d)

An extraordinary admission: probably only *in a democracy* is political philosophy, at least of the sort practiced in the *Republic*, possible. If political philosophy requires knowledge of human types and regimes, then (probably) only in a free-speaking democracy can the philosopher become sufficiently aware of human diversity to comprehend the nature of justice and injustice. Only in a democracy, Socrates suggests, would it be possible to "organize" or "construct" (*kataskeuazein*: 557d5) a "beautiful city." Only in a democracy, it seems, is it possible to imagine a regime that runs entirely against the grain of the one in which it is imagined. In other words, a democracy allows fundamental self-criticism.

This simple observation is the key to understanding the *Republic* as a qualified and cautious defense of democracy. Although the participants in the dialogue are undeniably cognizant of its blatant shortcomings, and so readily conceive of a radically antidemocratic alternative, their very doing so is itself compatible with and "probably" dependent upon being in a democracy.

A cluster of recent commentators have turned just this observation into the focus of their interpretation of the *Republic*. Euben, for example, drawing a "distinction between being a sympathetic if critical friend of democracy and being antidemocratic" (1996, 333), locates Plato squarely among the former. He does so because by his lights, philosophical dialogue itself both requires democracy and is intrinsically democractic. "Socrates not only assumes democracy as a context for his critique of politics, he elaborates democratic practices into a philosophical/political vocation"; as a prime example of the latter, each participant in a dialogue "is accorded the dignity and respect that ideally helped define democratic citizenship" (335). Euben's view here is considerably overstated, but its general sentiment is sensible. As mentioned above, radical self-criticism is permissible, perhaps even essential, in a democracy. Correspondingly, "dialectic," the name Euben gives to philosophical dialogue conceived in a broad (and hence ambiguous) sense, "demands that one be

willing to open oneself up to a refutation of one's life" (350). Indeed,
if, as Euben thinks, "democracy is debate about what democracy is,
then what better example can we have than . . . Socrates?" (335). (See
Barber 1996 for a critique of Euben.)

Philosophical dialogue, regardless of how strongly it criticizes the
political regime of democracy, itself instantiates crucial democratic
features.[1] First and foremost, as Monoson (1994) argues at length, it
does so because dialogue requires free or "frank speech," *parrhēsia*.
This legendary Athenian virtue, she writes, "is consistently and
closely associated with two things: criticism and truth telling. . . . [It
is] equated with 'telling the truth as one sees it'" (1994, 175). Consequently, it is required both to participate authentically in the Assembly and to engage in serious conversation with Socrates. In fact,
"Plato draws on the ideal of parrhesia . . . in his representation of the
practice of philosophy" (185). Thus, Monoson argues, "Plato's texts
defend the idea of parrhesia and appropriate this democratic strategy
of civic discourse for philosophy" (172). As I do, Monoson relies heavily on 557d to undercut the familiar notion of Plato as a fervent anti-
democrat: the passage "challenges the assumption that philosophy
and democracy are thoroughly at odds. . . . Democracy to some extent sustains an environment conducive to philosophy" (185). (See
Monoson 2000 for a thorough elaboration of this view.)

Saxonhouse puts a similar point thus: "Callipolis is not a democracy. . . . But the *Republic* . . . shows how the discourse among the
Platonic characters relies on democratic principles of engagement,
equality, and communal decision making. Philosophy as an activity
in which Platonic characters engage . . . has much more in common
with democracy that it does with aristocracy" (1996, 102). Indeed,
"democracies provide the bases for what Socrates cares most about:
the activity of philosophy and the education of the young" (90). From
these observations Saxonhouse does not infer that Plato is a defender
of democracy; she puts the point more tentatively: "Democracy is of
interest to Socrates" (90). Saxonhouse's caution comes from her understanding of the profoundly serious critique of democracy offered
in book 8, specifically its "dispensing a certain equality to equals and
unequals alike" (558c). In other words, with its extraordinary toler-

---

1. Samons 2001 argues that what I refer to as "democratic features" are not in fact
uniquely democratic but are characteristic of traditional Greek *polis* government in
general. His essay (and forthcoming book) is a useful corrective to many prevailing readings of Athenian democracy.

ance and "openness," democracy provides no resources for the rendering of strong value judgments. Indeed, this is precisely what leads to its downfall: "It remains incapable of discriminating against those who will undermine its openness—the tyrant" (Saxonhouse 1996, 113). By contrast, philosophy provides what democracy lacks: namely, "the capacity to make those judgments" (114) required to establish strong distinctions between human beings and political regimes.

Saxonhouse rightly emphasizes the ambiguity of Plato's response to democracy: although undeniably critical of it, he nonetheless "acknowledges the centrality of democracy for the pursuit of philosophy" (91). She formulates (quite precisely as I explain in the next section) the essential question posed by book 8 as follows: "Must one live in a democracy to dream of a Callipolis?" (100). The answer, according to Plato, is "probably" yes. To explain why, consider the following six components of Socrates' description of democracy in book 8.

(1) *Freedom of Speech.* "In the first place," Socrates says about the citizens of a democracy, "aren't they free? And isn't the city full of freeedom and free speech [*parrhēsia*: 557b5]?" This is the salient feature of a democracy that Mononson makes critical to her argument about Plato's defense of democracy. Citizens can say what they want to say. They can criticize their own regime and cook up schemes they think are better. They can, in short, enter into philosophy and, if they wish, articulate what they believe is a beautiful city in speech.

(2) *License.* "And isn't there license [*exousia*: 557b5] in it to do whatever one wants?" Not only can citizens speak freely; they can do whatever it is possible (*exesti*, from which *exousia* is derived), whatever is in their power, to do. There are legal limits, of course, but within them, citizens can act as they wish. They can, for example, travel freely, visit private homes, attend foreign religious festivals, and, if they choose, engage in philosophical dispute.

(3) *Eros Polymorphous.* Because of (1) and (2), a democracy allows for the "unleashing of unnecessary and useless pleasures" (561a). Its citizens can act on their impulses, attempt to fulfill their desires, allow themselves polymorphous expression of their own Eros. Unlike the Kallipoleans, citizens can marry and have sex with whomever they wish. Or they can refrain from sex altogether. They can participate in the Assembly and act on their love of

power, or they can pursue their love of wisdom. They can create beautiful statues, write plays, study mathematics, or dream of the Forms.

(4) *Privacy*. Socrates encapsulates this train of thought by saying, "And where there's license, it's plain that each man would organize [*kataskeuazoito:* 557b9] his life in it privately [*idian*] just as it pleases him." The word Bloom translates as "organize" is the same one used at 557d5: those who wish "to organize a city, as we were just doing"—that is, those who "construct" a city in speech—probably must live in a democracy whose "license" allows construction projects of all sorts to take place. Some are political, such as the construction of a political ideal. Others are aesthetic or theoretical. The key point is that the freedoms of democracy unleash the individual desires and urges on which one acts. In a democracy, citizens are free to *dream*.

The notion of privacy is especially important in light of an earlier remark Socrates made to Adeimantus. In book 6, when presenting what might be termed his "sociology of philosophy," he explained that in actual cities only a very small group of people ever become real philosophers. The reason is their skills—intelligence, discipline, the ability to defend a thesis and to refute competitors—are so highly valued by the city that, anachronistically put, potential philosophers are seduced into becoming highly paid lawyers. As a consequence, the few left to practice real philosophy are highly anomalous and so face great hostility from their fellow citizens. Indeed, "it's impossible," Socrates says, "that a multitude be philosophic . . . and those who do philosophize are necessarily blamed by them" (494a) because the "many" cannot "accept or believe that the fair itself is, rather than the many fair things, or that anything itself is, rather than the many particular things" (493e).

As discussed in the second section of chapter 2, philosophers are impelled by the unique erotic configuration of their souls to seek things themselves, to attach the intensive pronoun to the object of their desire (see 476a–b). This is precisely what the many (who can take Wittgenstein as their champion here) resent so passionately: the philosopher's contempt for the particular, for the ordinary. As a result, a philosopher must protect himself from "the madness of the many" (496c). He must keep quiet and mind his own business. "Seeing others filled full of lawlessness, he is content if somehow he himself can live his life here pure of injustice" (496d). In other words, he lives a private rather than a fully political life. (Compare *Apology* 32a.)

Of course, Kallipolis is designed to eliminate such privacy. Recall, however, the conclusion of the previous chapter: philosophy, conceived as a fully erotic enterprise, could not exist in Kallipolis, yet the *Republic*, taking place in a private home, is required for Kallipolis to come into being.

The notion of privacy returns dramatically at the very end of the dialogue. In the myth of Er (see this chapter's third section), Odysseus is the last to choose his type of life. He selects "the life of a private man" (620c6), which "he would have done . . . even if [he] had drawn the first lot" (620d). This story, needless to say, would surely be censored in Kallipolis, where identification of the private and public is complete.

Perhaps the most powerful expression of a democracy's affirmation of the private, and the one distinguishing it most sharply from Kallipolis, is this: it imposes on its citizens no "compulsion [*anangkēn:* 557e2] to rule." Those who want to divorce themselves from political activity in a democracy may do so—in stark contrast to the paradigmatically Kallipolean moment in the allegory of the cave when the liberated prisoners are compelled (*anangkasai:* 519c9) to return to the cave, there to participate fully in political affairs.

(5) *Diversity.* Because of a democracy's unleashing and toleration of the polymorphous manifestations of Eros, its citizens are diverse. Thus, Socrates describes democracy as "probably the "fairest [*kallistē*] of the regimes . . . just like a many-colored [*poikilion*] cloak decorated [*pepoikilmenon*] in all the hues, this regime, decorated with all dispositions, would also look fairest, and many perhaps . . . like boys and women looking at many-colored things [*ta poikila*] would judge this to be the fairest regime" (557c4–9).

This description is easily construed as negative: democracy seems the most beautiful of regimes but only to those boys and women seduced by its superficial gaudiness; it would not, the implication might be, seem so beautiful to someone experienced and knowledgeable. But it is advisable to resist such a conclusion. First, as the character of Glaucon suggests, youthfulness can generate a unique form of appreciation and insight. Second, as Saxonhouse (1997) has shown

exceptionally well, women are associated with philosophy throughout the *Republic*, so their affirmation of the "many-colored" regime
of democracy should not be taken lightly. Finally, and for the purpose
of this section most important, there is an unmistakable affinity between the "luxurious" or "feverish" (372e) city (which follows from
Glaucon's rejection of the "true" and "healthy" [372e] city in book 2)
and democracy. Just as Socrates offers a qualified approval of the former, Plato makes the same judgment on the latter.

Recall that the feverish city is brought into being by Glaucon's dissatisfaction with Socrates' first, very simple, and peaceful city. The
life available there, however stable and harmonious, is "without relishes" (372c) and so, by Glaucon's lights, is fit only for pigs. He in-
jects the ever expansive power of desire into Socrates' city and
thereby destroys it. The feverish city moves far beyond "the mere ne-
cessities we were talking about at first—houses, clothes, and shoes."
In this second city, "painting and embroidery [*tēn poikilian*] must
also be set in motion; and gold, ivory, and everything of the sort must
be obtained" (373a6–9). Both the feverish city and the democracy contain a wide diversity of pleasures, many of them quite useless. Furthermore, both are brought into being by similar causes. The former
originates with young men, "gripped by a love of change" (555e), who
"have intercourse with fiery, clever beasts" (559d); the latter is generated by Glaucon's desire to have his "relishes."

The vocabulary Socrates used to tell that story in book 2 is strikingly similar to the one he uses in describing the democracy. In both
passages (373a, 557c) he relies on *poikilian*, one of whose meanings
is certainly "diversity" (see Monoson 2000, 224, for a discussion of
this word). Both the feverish city and the democracy are hot, and
their heat generates a wildly variegated set of useless pleasures.
(The same word also describes both the desiring part of the soul at
588c7 as a "many-colored beast [*thēriou poikiliou*]," and the first
and widest whorl of the fixed stars at 616e9.) Note also the similar
uses of *pantodapa* at 373a4, 373b8 (there are "all sorts" of delights
in the feverish city), and 557c1, where Socrates states that in a democracy "all sorts [*pantodapoi*] of human beings come to be." As a
result, a democracy "contains all species [*panta genē*] of regimes"
(557d4) and thereby provides fertile ground for a would-be political
philosopher.

(To get ahead of myself: note that according to the myth of Er, a
human soul must make a choice of lives from a selection of patterns

"far more" numerous than the number of those choosing. Facing the chooser are "all varieties [*pantodapa*: 618a3] of human lives." Not surprisingly, then, Odysseus, widely traveled and well versed in the various ways of men, and in Homer famously characterized as *polutropos* ("man of many ways)," is superbly equipped to make the best of choices.)

The point is simple: where freedom thrives, Eros is unleashed, and as a consequence a diverse array of human beings, guided by their varied sense of pleasure and beauty, arise. Such diversity is "probably" a necessary condition for the *Republic* itself, since "it is probably necessary for the man who wishes to organize a city, as we were just doing, to go to a city under a democracy" (557d). In a democracy one can walk the streets, encounter the unexpected on a regular basis, and thereby be educated in the human drama.

To state the obvious: the very essence of Kallipolis is a design to eliminate such diversity. It is the most monocultural and rigid of regimes its music designed to "purge" (399e) the feverish city and thus restore it to the health and stability of Socrates' first city. Despite its fever, however, Socrates offers no objections to Glaucon's critique of his first city. Instead, he says, "All right, I understand. We are, as it seems, considering not only how a city, but also a luxurious city, comes into being. Perhaps that's not bad either. For in considering such a city too, we could probably see in what justice and injustice naturally grow in cities" (372e).

The feverish city, unlike the first, must confront the grim fact of war, about which Socrates says, "Let's not say whether war works evil or good" (373e4). Why is he so cryptic? Perhaps because war emerges from the same source as do art and philosophy: namely, the powerful desires unleashed feverishly in a realistically human city. War is born from spirit (*thumos*). And just as the philosopher-rulers will ultimately be chosen from the guardian/warrior class, so too is there an unbreakable, even if lamentable, connection between our best possibilities and our worst instincts to kill and plunder. Both arise from our erotic strivings. There is a "necessity" (373e) to go to war, a necessity that Glaucon later describes as erotic (458d).

In sum, the description of the feverish city is ambiguous. So too is Socrates' description of the democratic man: "He also lives along day by day, gratifying the desire that occurs to him, at one time drinking and listening to the flute, at another downing water and reducing; now practising gymnastic, and again idling and neglecting everything; and sometimes spending his time as though he were occupied in philosophy" (561c).[2]

This picture is hardly flattering. Still, Socrates does locate philosophy, however sporadic and inauthentic its appearance may be, in the soul of the democratic man (Cooper [1984, 9] notes this point). At the least, democracy admits the *possibility* of philosophy, for it allows the free expression of desire. From this it hardly follows that philosophy will safely flourish in a democracy or is impossible outside of it. The execution of Socrates obviously speaks to the first point, and the flourishing of Western philosophy before the advent of modern democracies addresses the latter. Indeed, in book 6 of the *Republic* itself (495b–e), Socrates provides his own "sociological" analysis of how a democracy can degrade philosophy.

Again, the key point must be expressed with some ambivalence: the *Republic* does not champion the unadulterated goodness of democracy but does find it the source of much that is potentially interesting. Like Glaucon's feverish city, and like war, it is home to both goods and bads—mostly bads. But when the fever is allowed to burn, sufficient heat can be generated to fuel the mad pursuit of the extraordinary.

One final way to put this point about diversity: it is no accident that the *Republic* is set in the Piraeus, a seaport teeming with people and gods from all around the Mediterranean and traditionally a hotbed of prodemocratic sentiment.[3] Of course, Kallipolis would sanitize and silence places like the Piraeus. Would it thereby eliminate the possibility of political philosophy itself? If so, who would be its ruler?

(6) Eros the Tyrant. One way of summarizing Socrates' critique of democracy in book 8, a critique that is quite serious, is simply to say that it leads to tyranny. The enormous premium democracy places on freedom and equality (562b) leads not only to an unleashing of the diverse manifestations of Eros, but also to a corresponding rejection of any form of authority designed to hold human desires in check (563d). As a result, in addition to being fertile ground for all sorts of human projects, democracy breeds the most ineffectual of rulers. Unless they are "very gentle," con-

2. Note that flutes, the instruments of Dionysus, are prohibited in Kallipolis (399d).

3. The implication is that the kind of chronological argument made by Vlastos (1991, 248–251), that book 1 is earlier than and therefore conceptually distinct from 2–10, is totally wrong.

straining the freedom-loving citizens not at all, they will be charged with being "oligarchs" (562d) or authoritarians. The rulers will thus attempt to please the many poor who keep them in power. They will, for example, "take away the substance of those who have it, and distribute it among the people." Since they themselves are motivated by their own self-interest, however, they will "keep the greatest part for themselves" (565a). The democratic city thus becomes a cauldron of pandering, competition, and corruption, with the majority of people placed at odds against the powerful and rich few. Eventually, the people will "set up some one special man as their special leader" (565c). They will turn to a demagogue, a man with an insatiable lust for power who promises to protect the interests of his constituency. After establishing a political base, he will go even further and, claiming that the rich present a threat to the poor, will demand and receive his own bodyguard (566b). He will attack his enemies. He will get his first taste of blood, and this will turn him into a wolf, into a tyrant. (565d)

Because it privileges freedom above all else, democracy nourishes the tyrant. Democratic citizens have the freedom to dream all sorts of dreams, including those most ruthless and shameless (572b, 574e). In turn, these become the waking activities of the actual tryant, the man whose desire for exclusive power has run wild. Democracy is "like a many-colored [*poikilion*] cloak decorated [*pepoikilmenon*] in all the hues," while "the tyrant's camp," dominated as it is by the ever expanding panoply of the tyrant's desires, is a "fair, numerous many-colored [*poikilion*: 568d6] thing."

Socrates' description of tyranny is firmly linked to his previous account of democracy by its singular emphasis on Eros. "A man," he says, "becomes tyrannic in the precise sense when, either by nature or by practice, he has become drunken, erotic and melancholic." Tyranny is a maddening of the soul; it is Eros unbowed by convention and law. And so it is that "Eros has from old been called a tyrant" (573b–c).

The picture Socrates draws of the tyrant is severely critical. Despite the appearance of being secure and free, he is in fact a slave to his desire for power (576a). In order to protect his position of authority he must, for example, "gradually do away with all of" his previous allies and earlier friends (567b). Indeed, he must eliminate all potential competitors from the city, and so he plots against anyone remotely like himself, anyone "who is courageous, who is great-minded, who is prudent, who is rich" (567c). Consequently, he is friendless (576a), surrounded only by lackeys, and in a constant state of fear (579e). The tyrant "can't go anywhere abroad or see all the things the other free men desire to see" (579b) because he fears assassination. He is the worst of rulers, one who fundamentally exploits his people because "he is always setting some war in motion, so that the people will be in need of a leader" (566e). He will even commit parricide, should doing so be advantageous for him (569b, 574c). He is riotously out of control, and he totally disregards law. All this is a consequence of his unbridled Eros at work: "Love lives like a tyrant within him in all anarchy and lawlessness" (574e).

Although there is no disputing the negative characterization of the tyrant, this section of the *Republic* is far more than a blanket condemnation. Only here does Socrates do justice to Eros, taking it up as an explicit theme and giving full voice to its richly dangerous, "limb-loosening" powers. From its covert introduction in book 1, when old Cephalus admiringly quotes Sophocles, through Glaucon's interruption of Socrates' first city in book 2 and Polemarchus's in book 5, through the thoroughly erotic description of the philosopher in book 6 generated by these interruptions, Eros has been gaining force. The failure of the marriage number to control sexual reproduction in book 8 culminates its shattering march through Kallipolis, and in book 9 it is, finally, directly confronted on its own terms. Eros is a tyrant. The dialogue has reached its third wave.

One clue to the philosophical importance of Socrates' discussion of tyranny and the tyrant is its length (562a–569c, 571a–580a). It equals almost exactly the total number of pages previously devoted to the timocracy (547d–550c), oligarchy (550c–555b) and democracy (555b–562a) combined. This textual detail signifies the sense in which tyranny animates and underlies all the previous regimes. Eros is intrinsic to political activity itself, for as Glaucon's second city of relishes demonstrates, politics is born from the expansive nature of desire.

At the beginning of book 9, Socrates states, "In my opinion we haven't adequately distinguished the kinds and numbers of the desires" (571a). Only now, with the honest acknowledgment of Eros as tyrant, is it possible to do so. As a result, this third wave of the *Republic* contains psychological resources far richer than those available in the first and the second. Specifically, Socrates revises the tripartite psychology of book 4. To do so, he begins with the familiar distinction between necessary and unnecessary desires. This division, of course, harks back to the transition from Socrates' healthy "city of utmost necessity" (369d) to Glaucon's "luxurious" and "feverish" city of "perfume, incense, courtesans and cakes" (372e–373a). Socrates then divides "the unnecessary pleasures and desires" into two categories: those "hostile to law" and those that are "better." The former "probably come to be in everyone," but "with the help of argument" they can be checked by the laws and the latter (571b). Even if checked, such repressed desires will often appear in dreams. This happens least of all to the most thoroughly self-controlled person (572b), but even he will never eliminate them entirely. "Some terrible, savage [*agrion*], and lawless form of desires is in every man, even in some of us who seem to be ever so measured. And surely this becomes plain in dreams" (572b). (Compare the use of *agrion* at 329c.)

Socrates' discussion of Eros the tyrant discloses the power of repressed desire, of rage, of incest (571d), of dreams. Its emergence thus demands a rethinking of the entire soul. The tripartite scheme of book 4, though a useful beginning and an informative reminder of the power of the arithmetical, was static and too flat. Its conception of desire was illustrated not by a story of a tyrant who "tastes of kindred blood" (565e) but by examples drawn from mathematics and the *technai*. Its version of the soul was locked into a single frozen moment by the Principle of Non-Opposition (PNO) and its "at the same time" condition. It could not develop, had no depth, no memory, suffered no repression, and did not dream. Because the book 4 scheme conceived of reason only as calculation and then separated it from desire, it could not account for the erotic madness implicit in the love of wisdom. It therefore has to be negated in order for philosophy to emerge. Hence, the second wave of the *Republic*, books 5–7, is "set into motion," and Socrates attempts to incorporate the philosophical soul into Kallipolis. With the injustice required to force the philosopher back into the cave, however, and the inability of the rulers to calculate the marriage number, this attempt fails. And so the *Republic* concludes with its third wave, books 8–10.

Central to the dialectical revision of the tripartite psychology is the reformulation of the three "parts" of the soul. "Just as a city is divided into three forms, so the soul of every single man also is divided into three" (580d). As opposed to what he presented in book 4, however, this time Socrates invokes an animating principle to unify the soul: "gain-loving" (*philokerdes*: 581a7), "victory-loving" (*philonikon*: 581b2), and "wisdom-loving" (*philosophon*: 581b9) replace desire, spirit, and calculation. In other words, by the time Socrates reaches book 9, he acknowledges that "we act with the soul as a whole" (436b), not by means of separate parts. "We" are, in other words, understood as essentially erotic beings striving in time—toward the future but burdened with a buried past—for what we love.[4]

To summarize this line of thought: a basic criticism of democracy is that it is fertile breeding ground for the tyrant. But since only by confronting the tyrant can Eros be given its due, this criticism must be reconceived. Yes, democracy is extremely dangerous, for it allows the demagogue to arm himself and then to threaten the city itself. (And it might execute the philosopher.) But no, Plato does not utterly condemn it. By tolerating the wild dreams and diverse flourishings of Eros the tyrant, by allowing its citizens to lead private lives, democracy offers fertile, even if precarious, ground for philosophy itself.

To approach the same point from a different angle: there is a potentially disturbing similarity between the tyrant and the philosopher. Both are immensely erotic and seek their satisfaction far beyond the ordinary. Unlike that of the philosopher, however, the Eros of the tyrant is unrestrained and so partakes not at all of "true friendship" (576a). His is an Eros savage with its own expansion. By contrast, philosophical Eros, informed as it is by the great and gentle suasions of arithmetic, is mad for what is utterly other than itself: that is, the stability of being and the unitary character of the Forms. For these reasons the condemnation of tyranny, and hence of democracy, contains within it a positive lesson about Eros, which is required for an understanding of the love of wisdom.

The point is solidified when Socrates says that the worst life is led by the man "who is tyrannic and doesn't live out a private life but has bad luck and is given the occasion to become a tyrant" (578c). This statement opens up the possibility of some sort of private tyranny which is (at least) superior to a public one (see 496d). Might

---

4. The difference between *philokerdes* and *philochrēmatos* (581a6) is inconsequential.

it be possible, for example, to be tyrannized in private by the *desire* for wisdom?

To conclude: Kallipolis is thoroughly repressive and antidemocratic and thus runs no risk of breeding a tyrant who subsequently would conquer the city. At the same time, however, it would render mute the very philosophical activity of the *Republic*. Since the *Republic* is a requirement for the coming-into-being of Kallipolis, the latter would silence not only the speakers and context from which it is generated but itself as well. In this sense, the *Republic*, understood in its entirety as a dialectical development, is a complex and qualified defense of democracy, "multiculturalism," and erotic "diversity." It must also be understood as superior to Kallipolis. Simply put, the *Republic* is a work of philosophy, and it is precisely philosophy that would starve, wither, and die in Kallipolis.

An obvious question should be directed at the argument I have presented: why would Plato go to so much trouble to have his Socrates construct Kallipolis, with its attendant tripartite psychology, if he is really out to subvert or revise it, if he is really out to defend democracy and diversity? Does my argument imply, as Burnyeat puts it, "that Plato disbelieved his own theory?" Does it attribute a radical irony to the *Republic*? If so, then has it unleashed a hermeneutical principle which, like the tyrannical soul, knows no restraints? Once irony is accepted as a mode of reading, is not the door left open to all kinds of "perversities," readings that turn the text upside down and make "hard [texts] . . . harder to understand and the easier ones . . . the most difficult of all" (Burnyeat 1985, 33)?

This kind of hostile, almost incredulous, response has long greeted any ironic reading of the *Republic*. The reading I offer, however, does not actually attribute irony to the dialogue.[5] Irony implies an outer surface, meant not to be taken seriously, which conceals an inner, seriously intended depth. The reading I propose is not ironic, principally because the kinds of revisions I have discussed take place *on the surface* of the dialogue itself, and the kinds of negations that follow are dialectical ones which, just as they revise, preserve what is negated in its partiality.

Kallipolis fails because it is internally unstable and must, therefore,

---

5. The one exception to this statement concerns the treatment of poetry in book 10. Here I agree with the conclusions reached by Charles Griswold (1981).

undermine itself. It needs to control Eros in all its manifestations (except the philosophical), and this it cannot do. These two statements simply report what transpires on the surface of book 8: the city in speech dissolves because its rulers fail to arrive at the mathematical eugenics needed to regulate sexual intercourse. Similarly on the surface are the other basic points discussed throughout this book. As Socrates explicitly says, "It is probably necessary for the man who wishes to organize a city, as we were just doing, to go to a city under a democracy" (557d). It is a fact that Socrates begins this dialogue by attending a *new* religious festival and then proceeds to banish all innovation. In book 9, Eros is condemned as a tyrant, but the central books of the dialogue are a digression generated specifically by Eros: that is, the objection concerning the communalization of sexual relations. Again on the surface of the text is the concluding myth with which Socrates urges Glaucon to gain knowledge of a wide diversity of human lives (618a)—a possibility not available to him in Kallipolis— and depicts Odysseus as choosing the very non-Kallipolean life of a private man (620c).

Finally, recall the last condition needed to make the city "in a way possible": every citizen over the age of ten must be sent into the country (541a). This clean slate is a logical requirement for a regime that aims to overcome systematically all the deficiencies of ordinary human life. It takes but a moment's thought, however, to realize that a regime run by a revolutionary avant-garde and children under the age of ten cannot possibly be maintained. And even if it could, it would be monstrous.

Still, if the *Republic* is a qualified defense of democracy and of the very diversity and innovation that Kallipolis condemns, why did Plato argue so indirectly? Why did he not produce a more straightforward work, perhaps something akin to a treatise by John Locke or John Stuart Mill?

Even if it is a breeding ground for philosophers, democracy is fraught with useless pleasures, softheaded liberality, ignorant rulers, and tyrannical dreams. As such, for Plato it *is* largely objectionable. Cumulatively, then, his judgment is complex. Because a democracy allows for the blooming of a hundred flowers and ten thousand weeds, it would be irrational not to criticize it. The spectacle of democracy, of rule by opinion rather than knowledge, is disheartening and *should* be a goad to the consideration of a better world. Therefore, to postulate an ideal city, one managed by knowledge rather than opinion, is altogether rational. A democracy, however, allows for the unfettered creation and consideration of ideal cities. But when an ideal is postulated, it becomes equally sensible to criticize it by, among other things, counting its cost. The *Republic*, precisely because it is a dialogue taking place in a democracy, because it creates and then ultimately criticizes its own creation, thus reflects and appropriately expresses the dialectical stress, the frustration, intrinsic to democracy.

The *Republic* is a work of extraordinary tension. In setting out the conditions under which perfect justice can come to be, it teaches that perfect justice is neither possible (the marriage number fails) nor desirable (we don't really want to exile everybody over ten). On the other hand, the dialogue affirms that concerned citizens and decent human beings long for justice; they desperately want the stupid killing, the senseless factionalism, the terrible inequality and unhappiness of political life to cease. The city Socrates and Glaucon construct *is* an ideal. In Kallipolis there is no internal strife, no power-mongering, no erotic triangles, no love of money. Self-interest collapses into the interest of the community. But if the longing for such an ideal were acted upon in a radical and consistent manner, if the attempt were made actually to implement it in deed—or even if only in speech—those conditions required for perfect justice and the elimination of human suffering and irrationality would themselves be insufferable. As Strauss melodramatically puts it, "Certain it is that the *Republic* supplies the most magnificent cure ever devised for every form of political ambition" (1978, 65). At the same time, it affirms the human impulses fueling such ambition.

The *Republic*, in which Kallipolis is both constructed and undermined, embodies this complex tension. Its dialectical development, in which an untenable—because excessively arithmetical—ideal is posited and then subverted, both expresses and mirrors it. But to say that is not to say it is ironic. The *Republic*, with its going up to Kallipolis and then back down again to tyranny, *in its entirety* and *as a dialogue* means exactly what it says. And, as Euben, Monoson, and Saxonhouse have argued, it does so in a way uniquely appropriate to and "probably" dependent on a democracy.

2. NARRATIVE PSYCHOLOGY

Only with the introduction of the tyrant does the *Republic* generate sufficient psychological steam to do justice to the human soul. Erotic at its core, moving forward in time while ever carrying its past, it (somehow) acts as a whole, not by means of separate parts. To express this revised understanding, Socrates requires a kind of account far different from the static, arithmetical, PNO-driven argumentation of book 4. The final third of the dialogue provides just that.

Books 8 and 9 tell the story of the succession of "mistaken" regimes—the timocracy, oligarchy, democracy, and tyranny—as well as their corresponding character types. At times, the account mentions actual historical regimes (e.g., Crete and Sparta at 544c), and some of the points it makes about the democracy may loosely correspond to democratic Athens. But it is surely not, nor is it intended to be, historically accurate (cf. Annas 1982, 300). On the other hand, because it does appeal to empirical observation and historical references, and because its twists and turns are so thoroughly informal (and perhaps even arbitrary), the account is manifestly not meant to be a theoretical endeavor either. Simply put, the two books are strange. As a consequence, for Annas at least, this section of the *Republic* is "irritating" and both "confusing and confused" (1982, 294). (Cooper is more sympathetic; for example, he invokes the "four bad kinds of persons" [1984, 13] to illustrate his thesis about Plato's psychology.)

The treatment of individuals in books 8 and 9 is as peculiar as their account of regimes. Consider, for example, the story of the timocrat (449c–550b). He begins as a boy impressed by "his father's arguments" on behalf of virtue and self-control, but he is also mindful of the bitter complaints of his mother and the servants, who criticize the father for his indifference to the real world of wealth and power. The boy is torn, "drawn by both of these influences." He settles his psychic conflict by opting for a middle path. He "doesn't have a bad man's nature, but has kept bad company," and so he has "turned over the rule in himself to the middle part"—namely, spirit. He becomes the timocrat.

This vignette has a plausible ring. Children exposed to parents in radical disagreement may well pursue an equilibrium state, a psychological compromise designed to please each parent. Obviously, however, such children may just as readily side with one parent rather than the other as a way to ease their stress. Faced with the difficulty of steering a course through the terror of parental conflict, a child may adopt any number of unpredictable strategies. In short, even if plausible, the story is neither formally persuasive nor demonstrably true.

This simple observation reveals what is basic to the account: it is not an argument; it is a story. It should thus come as no surprise when, at the outset of this stage of the dialogue (547a), Socrates invokes the Muse. The final two sections of this chapter—whose titles, "Narrative Psychology" and "Psychological Narrative," indicate their mutual dependence—examine the meaning of Plato's use of stories in books 8–10. They conclude with a strong claim: this final third of the *Republic* is indeed like a third wave. It culminates the series of dialectical swellings that begin in book 2 and get stronger with the intrusion of Eros in book 5. For most commentators, the apex of the dialogue is reached in the spellbinding descriptions of the Idea of the Good and the divided line in book 6. By contrast, I argue that it is a terrible mistake to denigrate books 8–10, for only here does Plato bring an adequate *logos* of the soul to light.

To explain, I return to the book 4 model of desire. It is digital. X either wants or does not want Y. If X does want Y, then X either goes after it or does not go after it. There is no in-between, no vacillation, no conflict, no depth. In a similar fashion, only two possible relations obtain between calculation and desire: the former either successfully subordinates the latter (e.g., the thirsty person does not drink because calculation determines that it would be harmful to do so) or fails to override it (someone drinks even knowing it to be wrong). This is an impoverished account. As books 8 and 9 clearly show, human desire is invariably murky. Timocrats, for example, desire honor, which becomes their guiding light—but only during the day, for "under cover of darkness [they] pay fierce honor to gold" (548a). In this story the timocrats are profoundly conflicted human beings, their waking desire for honor infected by their repressed desire for gold. As a result, they must strategize hard in order to achieve monetary gain as well as glorious victory. If they succeed, these seemingly virtuous men get rich. They end up with "storehouses and domestic treasuries" (548a) of their very own.

By contrast to book 4, in this story human desire does not relate to its object *hama*, "at the same time," as, for example, the "greater" would relate to the "less" (438b). Instead, the object of desire is obscure and, to mention the salient consideration found in the stories of books 8 and 9, changes from day to night. And it is this change, rather than some logical puzzle about wanting and not-wanting "at the same time," that is truly interesting.

Consider again what Socrates said about the third "part" of the book 4 soul—namely, "spirit." Recall that he arrived at it not by means of an argument but by the story of Leontius, who, walking up from the Piraeus, "noticed corpses lying by the public executioner and made himself turn away" (439e). Presumably, Leontius did so because he thought it was wrong to look at dead bodies. Finally, however, unable to control himself and "overpowered by desire," he gave in to the temptation to look. Having done so, he reprimanded himself: "Look, you damned wretches," he screamed at himself and his eyes, "take your fill of the fair sight" (440a).

Socrates apparently used this story to establish the presence of a psychological capacity able to ally itself with calculation against the impulses of desire. But the story is far too complex to accomplish this simple task, and in being so it suggests (proleptically) what is limited about the tripartite account. First, what exactly did Leontius want? He wanted to see (439e9). To see what? Was he seeking titillation? Was he, as legend has it, some sort of necrophiliac? Or was he, as so many of us are, profoundly curious about the look of death? Was he seeking to remind himself of his mortality, to force himself to imagine his own demise? In other words, did his desire to look token an urge for a kind of self-knowledge (an urge that could not be accounted for by the conception of desire operative in book 4)? And why, really, did he become so angry with himself after he did look? Was it only because he thought he had done something shameful, as the story suggests? But perhaps Leontius's shame was uncomfortably mixed with desire. Perhaps the presence of death upset him in ways he himself was unable to fathom, and he lashed out blindly at himself without knowing why.

The point is this: even if the Leontius story seems to be offered as evidence of a third, separable part of the soul, it is too rich, too realistic, to accomplish its putative task.[6] Far from demonstrating that the soul is an object divisible into three countable parts, the story hints at the very limitations of the tripartite account. Again, Socrates himself alludes to these limitations when he asks whether we act not with separable parts but "with the soul as a whole" (436b). In doing so, he points forward to books 8 and 9.

To reiterate an old complaint: despite relying on critical passages from book 9 (especially 580–81) in order to bolster Plato's psychology, few commentators (with the notable exception of Jonathan Lear 1997) have taken sufficient advantage of the great resources of books

---

6. Similarly, the reference to an Odysseus story at 390d is too complex for its purpose.

8 and 9 on this score. Fewer still have reflected on the question of what sort of book the *Republic* is such that later material revises and supplements earlier. And none, as far as I know, have wondered why, in these late stages of the dialogue, Socrates turns to narrative to finish his job. The reason for this last omission is simple, and again Annas is typical: although books 8 and 9 "have been admired for their literary power . . . they leave a reader who is intent on the main argument unsatisfied and irritated. Plato's procedure is both confusing and confused." Big chunks of the two books can be dismissed because they are literary rather than philosophical (Annas, 1982, 294).[7] I defend the opposite view: precisely *because* they are literary these books represent a most valuable dimension of Plato's psychology. Stories can tell much about who we are in ways arguments based on the PNO and its "at the same time" condition never can.

Four specific features of books 8 and 9 illustrate their narrative quality: (1) Socrates' use of informal vignettes, little stories, to propel his account of the succession of regimes; (2) his use of "psycho-biographies" to describe the individuals; (3) the blurry lines he deliberately draws between regimes and individuals; (4) the ample "psychological space" he provides for a soul whose nighttime dreams and repressed desires drive it forward during the day.

(1) The timocracy, Socrates says, favors leaders who are "naturally more directed to war than to peace" (547e). But such men have a private side which they shield from the public that honors them: "Under cover of darkness [they] pay fierce honor to gold" (548a). Presumably because they have won the spoils of war, they are able to furnish their homes lavishly: "They will have walls around their houses, exactly like private nests, where they can make lavish expenditures on women and whomever else they might wish" (548a). The timocrat is thus a sly and stealthy character who must, as a result, suffer conflict and anxiety. His strong desires cannot possibly be fulfilled because they are expressible only under the cover of darkness. His day time public self is at odds with the money-loving man he is becoming at night.

Socrates describes in some detail how the timocrat comes into being. He is the son of an aristocratic—hence, unworldly—father (550a) and a grasping, dissatisfied, complaining mother (549c–d). In addition, the future timocrat is exposed to the exhortations of his

---

7. This isn't entirely fair. In fact, Annas (1982) makes her usual intelligent observations about this section.

mother's allies, the "domestics" (549e), who echo the mother's complaints about the father.

Socrates introduces this passage (549c–550b) by explicitly admitting its limitations. The timocrat, he says, "somehow [*pōs*: 549c2]
comes to be in the following manner." Bloom misses the indefinite-
ness of the *pōs* by translating, "And this is how he comes into being."
Bloom's "this" suggests a tight explanation of a psychological development. Whereas Socrates himself actually softens his account when
he begins it: "Sometimes [*eniote*] he is the young son of a good father."
Rather than offering a strict explanation of the timocrat's genesis, he
tells what is at best a "likely story." As such, it begins with a standard
narrative opening: "Once upon a (i.e., an indefinite) time . . ."

Socrates does not characterize his account as a strict explanation
or theory. This measure of self-awareness should be reassuring, for
only by understanding the passage as an informal narrative, whose
moves are bound not by the bonds of necessity but by probability, will
the passage make good sense. Without this understanding it may well
leave a reader like Annas "unsatisfied and irritated." She was, I assume, irritated by the apparently arbitrary moves of the story. Where
in the world, for example, did the future timocrat's conniving mother
and her yapping domestics come from? The answer: from Socrates'
imagination. He is sketching a believably fictional household.[8] A narrative is composed of particular characters acting within the contin-
gencies of their specific narrative context. Such particularity need not
be philosophically defended; it only needs to ring true. Socrates' vignette achieves just such plausibility. Annas's irritation would be
warranted only if Socrates were trying to present an argument.

In describing the oligarch, Socrates offers additional insights into
what began to emerge, during the description of the timocrat, as the
self-defeating character of money love. He begins by asserting that
"virtue [is] in tension with wealth, as though each were lying in the
scale of a balance always inclining in opposite directions" (550e). Presumably, the earlier sections of the *Republic* count as a massive argument on behalf of this proposition. At this point in book 8, however,
it is "verified" only by anecdote.

As the oligarch emerges from the timocracy, he counts money as
the first and best of all things. He "puts the desiring and money-loving
part on the throne" (553c) and subordinates all other aspects of his life

8. The household Socrates sketches could fit well in a comedy.

to it. As a result, he becomes "stingy and a toiler" (554a5). Those who place money at the pinnacle of their psychic hierarchy will dedicate themselves to making lots of it. The paradoxical dilemma of money, however, is that when such dedication bears fruit, when success is achieved and lots of money is made, the result is not pleasure but psychological discomfort. The money is there, but it cannot be spent without threatening the state of mind responsible for earning it. The impulse of the money-lover is thus not to spend but only to make more (useless) money. The oligarchical personality works constantly in order to expand his stash, and then fearfully hoards it.

Because such people resist extravagance and "unnecessary desires" (558d), they might seem to exhibit the virtue of moderation. In fact, however, an oligarchic man refrains from spending not because he holds higher values in greater regard but because when faced with the prospect of spending, "he trembles for his whole substance" (554d). In other words, because the money-lover has devoted so much psychic energy to toil and so closely identifies himself with the money that results, spending it feels like self-annihilation. Money is therefore the most withering of human preoccupations. Since it has no intrinsic worth, its only value is in its being spent, but this the money-lover fears to do. The result is a "squalid" (*auchmēros*: 554a10) man who is "dried" out because he is incapable of anything but worrisome toil.

Of course, nothing about the human soul or money logically or empirically necessitates the behavioral complex sketched above. It is possible to imagine a Bill Gates cheerfully spending billions. At best, therefore, the sketch Socrates offers is a likely story, perhaps ringing true to some of us about some wealthy people we have known. At the least, however, money does represent a psychological danger, and so Socrates' story may be counted as a cautionary tale. In this sense it bears some similarity to, for example, Ovid's story of Midas. Granted a wish by Bacchus, Midas chooses that all he touches will turn to gold. Despite its initial allure, his is "a choice that seemed a boon, but proved a bane," for even the food he tries to put into his mouth turns "hard and stiff," inedible and dire (*Metamorphoses* 9.100–125). Socrates' description of the oligarch, I suggest, is more akin to Ovid's myth than it is to an argument.

(2) Socrates announces that there are four soul types corresponding to the four mistaken regimes: "It is necessary that there also be as many

forms of human characters as there are forms of regimes" (544d6–7). Instead of simply articulating such "forms," however, in each case Socrates tells a developmental story. The example cited above works again. In 548d–550c, the putative discussion of the timocratic man, the reader is led to expect a formal articulation of a soul type. Instead, this section treats the genesis of such a man from childhood, when he was the son of an aristocratic father (544e) and a money-loving mother (549d). It is therefore really a mini-*Bildungsroman* in which the future timocrat is initially depicted as a child feeling the terrible brunt of parental conflict.

The pattern is consistent. The passage apparently intended to articulate the formal character of the oligarch (553b–555b) is actually the tale of a boy who watches in horror as his honor-loving father squanders the family fortune. As he matures, he vows not to let this happen again: "Humbled by poverty, he turns greedily to money-making" (553c). The democratic man begins as a boy whose father is rich but stingy, as well as uneducated. When a young man so carelessly reared is exposed to worldly temptations, he succumbs. He "has intercourse with fiery, clever beasts who are able to purvey manifold and subtle pleasures" and thereby "begins his change from an oligarchic regime within himself to a democratic one" (559d–e). Finally, the tyrannical man as a boy is raised by "democrats"—that is, in the heady atmosphere of complete freedom. As a result, "he is drawn to complete hostility to law." Experimenting with every form of desire, he becomes tyrannized by Eros, by the strongest of unnecessary desires. He wants everything. He even steals from his parents (574b).

These little stories have miniature plots unfolding through time. For Socrates, it seems, a *logos* of a soul type is a *logos* of a soul's coming-to-be, its history or story. To prefigure an argument soon to follow: the passage of time is essential to the conception of the soul in books 8 and 9. As a result, the plot-driven and diachronic narrative is the appropriate mode of expressing it. As Ricoeur puts it, "What is ultimately at stake in the case of the structural identity of the narrative . . . is the temporal character of human existence" (1984, 3). Correspondingly, "narratives . . . are the modes of discourse appropriate to our experience of time . . . and time experience, on the other hand, is the ultimate referent of the narrative mode" (1991, 107). On this score, the contrast with arguments governed by the PNO, whose "at the same time" condition freezes the flow of time into a single, logical moment, is sharpest.

(3) When Socrates states, "It is necessary that there also be as many forms of human characters as there are forms of regimes" (544d), he seems to be announcing a basic pattern of the whole account. Since "there are five arrangements of cities, there would also be five for the soul of private men" (544e). He will "consider first the regime" and then "consider the like man" (545b). These prefatory remarks lead the reader to expect a story with five distinct chapters, each with two sections. Chapter 1A has, presumably, already been completed in the creation of "Kallipolis" (527c2), the perfectly just city in speech. Correspondingly, chapter 1B would be the account of the perfectly just individual human being found in earlier books. The story should thus have four remaining chapters, each with two parts, to cover the four mistaken regimes and their four representative souls.

This expectation is not fully met, for the boundaries between both chapters and their subdivisions are regularly blurred. For example, 547c–548d "should" be a discussion of the timocratic regime (in other words, chapter 2A). In fact, however, this passage tells more about the character of timocratic men. As already discussed, despite their public manifestation of spirit and their devotion to war and victory, in private they love money and are terribly stingy (548b). Clearly, Socrates is here describing not a political regime but the development of a psychological type. It is subtly jarring when, at 548d6, he asks, "Who, then, is the man corresponding to this regime?" What, if not such a man, has just been described?

Another example of thwarted expectations is this: after describing the democratic man (558c–562a), Socrates states that "the fairest regime and the fairest man would be left for us to go through, tyranny and the tyrant" (562a). In other words, he seems here to announce a clear chapter break, a transition from 3B (democratic man) to 4A (tyrannical regime). But far from fulfilling this promise, Socrates continues to talk about democracy. For example, it is in this section, not the preceding one, that he discusses the primacy of freedom in a democracy (562b–c) and goes on to elaborate its consequences for various institutions, such as education (563a).

As he progresses in the "chapter" on tyranny, it becomes unclear whether Socrates is talking about the regime or the man (which itself is a powerful comment on the nature of tyranny). At 566d, for example, he says, "Let us . . . go through the happiness of the man and the city." He then proceeds to discuss the man. Again at 571a, however, he seems to commence a new section with "Well . . . the tyrannic man himself remains to be considered."

These features of books 8 and 9 reinforce a point that Lear has articulated exceptionally well: "Plato's is a developmental psychology" that offers "a dynamic account of the psychological transactions between inside and outside a person's soul, between a person's inner life and his cultural environment" (1997, 61). In other words, the individual is not a self-contained psychological unit—not a "thing," as Penner (1990, 105) would have it—but a dynamic being capable of both "internalizing" influences from the culture and "externalizing" itself, thereby helping to shape that culture. The result is a developmental process, not a static structure. But Lear does not make the point that I wish to emphasize: a narrative is required in order to express such a view of the soul. Since there is no impermeable line between the inside and outside of the soul—that is, since the soul is the ever changing locus of interactions between inside and outside—a precise and formally structured theory would be an inadequate vehicle for psychology.

(4) The key dynamic, the motive force, in effecting the transition from one regime to the next is supplied by the repressed desires of the individuals, by what goes on privately "in" their souls. A good example remains the timocrat who, despite his public display of devotion to civic honor, worships gold and silver while he is home at night. The timocrat spends much of his time alone in "psychic space." His son, the oligarch, will eventually enter this space and expose it to the public. Or consider an example Lear describes: the rise of the democratic man. His father, the oligarch, represses his unnecessary appetites, "but because he has not had a proper upbringing, because he has not experienced or internalized true culture, these appetites must be held in place by . . . brute force." As a result, the oligarchic father creates for his family a "micro-culture" embodying "contradictory demands." Within the family, there is the demand to be frugal. "But, on the other hand, the oligarchical father encourages prodigality outside the family. By lending others money and encouraging wastefulness, he hopes eventually to acquire their property" (Lear 1997, 76–77). No wonder, then, that the oligarch's son is suscep-

tible to the lure of the unnecessary desires that come to characterize the democracy. His repressed desires wait only to be triggered.

In a similar fashion, dreams become pivotal in these stories. The timocrat, for example, surely dreams of riches and thereby gives rise to his oligarchical son. Consider also the transition from democracy to tyranny. To introduce this "chapter," Socrates first divides desires into the necessary and unnecessary. Among the latter, some are lawful and some are not. Some of the latter "are checked by the laws and the better desires, with the help of argument" (571b). Others, however, "wake up in sleep when the rest of the soul . . . slumbers." In dreams the soul "doesn't shrink from attempting intercourse . . . with a mother or with anyone else at all—human beings, gods, and beasts" (571c). The democratic man dreams of unbridled desire, of polymorphous perversity, but only the tyrant lives out these dreams in waking reality: "Once a tyranny was established . . . what he had rarely been in dreams, he became continuously while awake" (574e; see also 576b).

Not only sexual desires awaken in dreams. For example, Adeimantus, upon hearing the description of the wild freedom found on the streets of a democracy (563c), reveals his fears of such chaos and reports that he has often had nightmares about it (563d). His is an austere, highly disciplined soul that dreams not of sex but of order. Or consider Socrates' own remark at 443b. After completing the book 4 analogy of the tripartite city and soul, he says, "That dream of ours has reached its perfect fulfillment." The specific dream Socrates refers to here began with his initial insight, expressed in book 2 (370b), that the organizing principle of Kallipolis should be "one man, one art," or simply "one one" (*heis mian*: 370b6). This dream of ones, of arithmetical stability, reaches its fulfillment in book 4 with the conception of a perfectly stable city of three distinct classes and an analogous soul of three parts.

In sum, the soul is alive with an extraordinary array of dreams. Future tyrants dream of unleashing their unnecessary desires. Others, like Adeimantus, have nightmares about disorder. Socrates, like the mathematicians who dream of being (533b), dreams of arithmetical stability, of orderly units fitting together neatly. Indeed, Kallipolis itself is like a dream (*enupnion*: 443b7). The polymorphous, dreaming soul, replete with private fantasies and repressed desires, supplies the fuel for the progression narrated in books 8 and 9, a progression that the static, tripartite Kallipolean psychology of book 4 cannot possibly account for.

Because the soul is essentially temporal, and, as Socrates suggests, "we act with the soul as a whole" (436b1) rather than with individual parts, the structural and static account in book 4 is inadequate. As Diotima explains in the *Symposium*, human action is generated by desire, which itself is comprehensible only through an understanding of its temporality. We desire an object we are aware of lacking, and then we move toward it. Even if we should attain the object (such as, to use Diotima's example, health), we will desire to maintain its possession into the future as well (*Symposium* 200d). No object completely satisfies or stops us dead in our tracks. For us, there is no rest. Here today, gone tomorrow is our motto, certainly not the "one one" of the first wave. We may well desire stability, but we will not attain it. For us, all is negation: not today but maybe tonight. And so it is that we desire, because we do not possess, the pure, positive presence of the Form.

In a parallel fashion, as the stories of books 8 and 9 illustrate, we cannot escape our familial past. We carry with us the rantings of our fathers and imprecations of our mothers.

A story gives voice to this self-consciously temporal experience. A character moving through the sequence of events constituting a plot (*muthos*) exemplifies the inevitable changes and, hence, inevitable conflicts of a human life.[9] The psychology of book 4 is widely interpreted by commentators as Plato's attempt to explain just such conflicts. Many, such as Penner (1990, 96), read it as Plato's rectification of Socrates' "earlier" repudiation of *akrasia* (in, for example, the *Protagoras*). The bipartition of the soul into calculation and desire seems to explain how a person can either control his thirst by refusing to drink, or fail to control it by being overpowered by his desire. Such an account has its merits, as Penner thinks, but it does no justice to human conflict occurring through time. For not only, indeed not primarily, does the phenomenon of wanting to drink and refusing to drink "at the same time" need to be explained; indeed, human beings never really live "at the same time," in a frozen, logical moment, at all. Instead, and far more important, what it means to have dinner at home with a miserly father who preaches frugality but actually loves gold, and then to hit the streets at night to consort with "fiery, clever beasts" (559d), needs to be explained. What is it to dream about having sex with "human beings, gods, and beasts" (571d) and then to act modestly during the day?

9. For *muthos* as "plot," see Aristotle *Poetics* 6.

It is telling that "beast" is used in both passages above, for the human soul, like the "spirit" described by Diotima, is "in between" the beastly and the divine (*Symposium* 202e). (And, of course, the "multifold beast" is used to represent desire in the "slightly nightmarish" nonpicture of the soul in book 9.) As such, it is necessarily unstable. To be itself, it must unfold in different configuations over the course of time. The human soul is potentially beast or god, and at different times it lapses into one or aspires to the other. A story featuring a particularized character who does things, changes his mind, gets sick, has dreams, proposes philosophical theories, gets angry, is required to express fully this dimension of the soul. A plot is driven by contingent events to which the character responds. A good story, which is a work of the imagination, shows both conflict and, sometimes, its resolution. In this sense, narrative does justice to the soul understood as a working, temporal whole, to the soul understood as a life.

There are at least three reasonable objections to what I have just presented.

(1) In book 10, Socrates argues that the soul is immortal, and not essentially temporal (608d–612a). Not least of the many difficulties in this passage is the formulation of the argument's conclusion. To "see" the soul in its immortal splendor one must look

> to its love of wisdom, and recognize what it lays hold of and with what sort of things it longs to keep company on the grounds that it is akin to the divine and immortal and what is always, and what it would become like if it were to give itself entirely to this longing. . . . And then one would see its true nature—whether it is many-formed or single-formed, or in what it is and how. But now, as I suppose, we have fairly gone through its affections [*pathē*] and forms in its human life. (611e–612a)

Socrates distinguishes between what has been said up to "now" (612a5; see also 611b6, c2, c5, c6) and some other account to be given "then" (612a3). The former has articulated the "affections and forms" of the soul in its "human life." The latter would presumably capture its purely rational and divine aspect. But to what exactly does Socrates refer? Does the account up to "now" point to the tripartite scheme of book 4? This seems plausible, because Socrates promises that in the subsequent account one "would see [the soul's] true nature"—specifically, "whether it is many-formed or single-formed." Since the tripartite soul is obviously many-formed, it might seem that Socrates here repudiates his earlier psychology and, in a fashion similar to that of the *Phaedo*, claims that the soul is in fact simple. Or perhaps the account up to "now" refers only to the stories of the soul presented in books 8 and 9: that is, to the accounts of unjust, "mistaken" individuals. If so, then what will be said "then" about the soul's true nature and its immortality could refer to the entire tripartite soul, but only as it is instantiated in a perfectly just human being. In short, the debate hinges on what exactly Socrates claims to be immortal. Is it the entire tripartite soul, or only the philosophical part of the soul (Szlezák 1976)? Especially when commentators attempt to harmonize this passage with statements made about the soul in the *Phaedrus*, *Phaedo*, *Timaeus* (41c, 69c, 90a–d), *Statesman* (309c), and *Laws* (713e), the debate becomes extraordinarily thick. (See Szlezák 1976 for a good overview.)

The following proposal will allow me to remain neutral on this highly vexed passage. The two accounts Socrates mentions, the one up to "now" and some other, might be roughly described as the "theoretical" and the "phenomenological." In the first, one attempts to "see" (*theasasthai*: 611c1) the soul "as it is in truth, not maimed by community with body and other evils." In this pure and simple condition the soul would "keep company" with "what is always" (611e3). But such a "seeing" of the soul is not in itself a complete psychology, because it would not account for the "affections," the experiences, the sufferings, the *phenomena* of human life. Precisely these have been expressed and given up to "now" in the *Republic*. As Socrates puts it, "Now we were telling the truth about [the soul] as it looks [*phainetai*] at present" (611c6–7). Note well his use of "truth": the account of an earthbound, polymorphous, erotic, suffering soul has been phenomenologically adequate. Even if the soul is immortal and lives on (in either a single-formed or a many-formed state) after death, the *Republic* has told a truthful story about the experiences, the *pathē*, of being human.

But what portion of the *Republic* has actually told this story? Is it the tripartite psychology of book 4, which allows for a rational part to be separated and perhaps to live forever, or the narrative psychology of books 8 and 9, in which a complex soul works as a whole through time? In fact, it is both. Plato's psychology weaves together two strands. First, it expresses an extraordinary commendation of the human capacity for philosophy: that is, for the spirited affirmation of and the disciplined acting upon the "longing" (611e2) and "impulse"

(611e4) for "what is always" (611e3). Second, it discloses the most sensitive understanding of the temporal, conflicted, and always eroticized origin and context of all human urges. Philosophers may "long to keep company" with the divine, but they are human. They may seek to transcend the passage of time and reach the dry stability of the Forms, but in doing so they seek to lift themselves "out of the deep ocean" (611e5), the murky fluidity of human life, in which they dwell. Platonic psychology, exhibited best in the entirety of the *Republic*, tells both sides of the story.

To summarize: even if Socrates purports to prove the immortality of the soul in book 10, and even if he targets the soul as a simple, purely rational entity, his doing so would not jeopardize my argument. The major purpose of books 8 and 9 is to provide a psychology richer than the one articulated in book 4. It requires narrative, for the phenomena of human experience are essentially temporal and never occur "at the same time."

(2) Even granting the description of the soul as essentially temporal and conflicted, one might claim that it is nonetheless possible for a "psychoanalytical" theory to capture its nature. Furthermore, one could argue—as perhaps Lear (1997) would—that despite the tentative and fledgling character of his psychology in the *Republic*, Plato himself is blazing the trail to construct such a theory. I disagree. This is because of the inextricable role particularity plays in the Platonic dialogues. To explain, I return to Wittgenstein's well-known comments about Socrates.

Wittgenstein complains bitterly about Socrates' asking, "What is knowledge?" in the *Theaetetus*. The what-is-it question betrays the philosopher's "craving for generality," his "contemptuous attitude towards the particular case." It thus reveals a deep confusion about general terms (such as "knowledge")—namely, the inclination "to think that there must be something in common" in all particulars—and an overreliance "in our usual forms of expression" on the notion that the man who has learned a general term, say "leaf," "has thereby come to possess a kind of general picture of leaf." In general, the what-is-it question mimics the preoccupation with science, which becomes "the real source of metaphysics," which "leads the philosopher into complete darkness." By contrast, Wittgenstein recommends "concrete cases," which "alone could have helped [Socrates] to understand the usage of the general term" (Wittgenstein 1965, 18–19).

There is a profound and unintended irony in this statement. Wittgenstein's complaint is itself a generalization: contempt for particulars, he tells us, is very bad . . . in general! In wonderful contrast, Plato himself, the putative champion of universals, situates all assertions in a thoroughly particularized context. There are no general claims in the Platonic dialogues. There are only characters, often drawn in stunning detail, who occasionally make abstract claims. Even if in the *Republic*, for example, Socrate s expresses his distaste for those who wallow in particulars—the "lovers of sights" who are unable to "see and delight in the nature of the fair itself" (476b)—he does so at a specific moment, to specific interlocutors.

(A similar argument might be used against Aristotle's critique of Plato. His "practical wisdom" is supposedly a knowledge of particulars [*Nicomachean Ethics* 6.8.5], and this is the root of his most basic objections to Plato [1.6]. In other words, for Aristotle as for Wittgenstein, Platonism is infected with an excessive craving for the universal. Once again, however, it must be noted that Aristotle's critique itself takes place in a nonparticularized, contextless vacuum. His is a single voice speaking the general truth of the matters at hand. In other words, he takes up practical wisdom itself in a thoroughly theoretical manner.)

The Platonic dialogue contains and expresses a fundamental tension within the soul between the universal and the particular. Our souls are tightly strung wires, suspended between the universality of Form and the particularlity of experience, between *logos* and *muthos*, between time and eternity, the divine and the beastly. We are contingent beings located in a particular time and place, and desiring beings who wish to jump out of time. A theoretical psychology governed by the PNO, such as that found in *Republic* 4, cannot do justice to the richness of the human soul.

(3) Since narrative is a necessary component of psychology, stories somehow tell the truth about the human soul. But does this hold for all stories? Aren't there really bad, utterly uninformative stories? Of course. How, then, can one tell the difference between a better and a worse, a more and a less revealing story? Indeed, since narrative is fictional, how can there be a true or a false story?

This is a powerful objection. Plato, however, can accommodate it because he understands that narrative in and of itself is not sufficient. Instead, the story must appear within a context substantially composed of logical argumentation. Indeed, this blend of *muthos* and *logos* is the heart and soul of the Platonic dialogue. If the structural, PNO-governed account in book 4 is not sufficient, neither are the stories of books 8 and 9. They must work together. The "truth" of the narrative becomes visible only as a complement to the structural account. This is why, despite its inadequacies, book 4 is an integral "moment" in the dialectical development of the *Republic*. It too helps tell us who we are. There is, in the human soul, a desire for and intellectual access to stability and formal structure, and in precisely the same manner that the human experience of time and negation must be accounted for, so too must these. The final result is the Platonic dialogue understood as a hybrid, a blend of two nearly opposite intellectual tendencies. Rosen calls them "the poetic and mathematical aspects of philosophy" (1988, 103). Stories, then, can be "true," but only if appropriately located in a complex context in which they are complemented by logical argument.

Precisely this blend is the enormous achievement of Plato's *Republic*. It must be read as a whole, with books 4 and 8 and 9 working together. There is a structural account as well as a dialogue surrounding it, neither of which is dispensable. Just as it is valid to say of oneself, "My desire got the better of me," so is it necessary to have a tripartite scheme. But such a scheme is truthful only if it is situated in a context that bespeaks its limitations. Only a proper juxtaposition of *arithmos* and Eros can accurately reflect the nature of the human soul. The tripartite arithmetical account is atemporal, governed by the PNO and the "at the same time" condition; the narrative account operates with a soul conceived as essentially temporal, indifferent to the PNO. Both accounts are needed, for human beings, spanned as they are between beast and god, both live in time and aspire to leap out of time.

Recall that Socrates began his treatment of the three "parts" of the soul in book 4 with a caveat:

> Know well, Glaucon, that in my opinion, we'll never get a precise grasp of [the soul] on the basis of procedures such as we're now using in the argument. There is another longer and further road leading to it. But perhaps we can do it in a way worthy of what's been said and considered before. (435d)

There are two roads toward or ways of articulating the soul. The one employed in book 4 is explicitly said to be adequate, but only on the basis of the sort of argumentation offered up to that point in the

Republic. As argued above, this argumentation is limited by the need to implement the city-soul-letter analogy, the device used to *facilitate* the conversation with Glaucon and Adeimantus, and by the PNO, stated at 436d, almost immediately following the caveat. But what, then, would the longer road be? Of course, there is no way to know with certainty. Some commentators think this is a reference to the longer story of the Forms found in book 6. I offer a very different proposal: the longer way is an account of the soul in which the authority of the PNO is affirmed but also limited. It includes both a structural or logical scheme and an acknowledgment of the essential and disruptive role played by Eros and the passage of time. The latter becomes the plot-driven narrative, the story, and it is the core of books 8 and 9. But why is this road "longer"? Because, as just suggested, it cannot exist in and of itself. The narrative and the formal argument must be juxtaposed, interpenetrate, become integrated. The result is the immensely complicated, hybrid work known as the Platonic dialogue. In other words, the longer way is the *Republic* itself understood as a totality, as a dialectical blending of story and formal argumentation which holds both together in a precarious unity.

To close this section, I return again to the extraordinary "nonpicture" of the soul that Socrates draws in book 9. First, he instructs his listeners to conjure up an image of desire as a "single visible form [*idean*] for a many-colored [*poikilou*], many-headed beast, that has a ring of heads of tame and savage beasts and can change them and make all of them grow from itself" (588d). Second, he asks that a lion represent spirit. Third, in a striking but finally unsurprising move, a human being serves to symbolize reason. Most striking, however, is the final direction Socrates gives: "Then mold about them on the outside an image of one—that of the human being" (588d).

What Socrates asks us to "see" (588b10) cannot in fact be seen. As Annas puts it (1982, 319), it is "visually incoherent," for it is not a form, a "look," at all. A human exterior conceals within it a human being, a lion, and a many-headed beast. The human being within would presumably also contain a human being, a lion, and a many-headed beast. And so on. With this, the static, tripartite structure of book 4 is gone, replaced by a self-moving soul which (like Glaucon's feverish city) is in continual self-expansion. This is the soul articulated by the stories of books 8 and 9.

3. PSYCHOLOGICAL NARRATIVE

Poetry, specifically the made-up stories (*muthoi*) of books 8 and 9, is required in order to complete the task of giving a philosophical *logos* of the temporal and erotic character of the human soul. As a result, a crisis is reached in the dialectical development of the *Republic*. If philosophy is the project of giving a rational account, then doesn't the infiltration of poetry represent a form of compromise, degradation, or pollution? If philosophy requires poetry, then what finally differentiates the one from the other? The task facing Socrates in book 10 is thus to distinguish poetry from philosophy, for although the latter is crucially dependent on the former, they cannot be identical.

This reading of the *Republic*, I propose, will solve one of its great riddles. Why does Socrates abruptly and without explanation return to the theme of poetry in book 10, and then proceed to change drastically the terms of his earlier critique?

Socrates opens book 10 by shifting his position on the role of imitative poetry. In book 3 the "unmixed imitator of the decent" (397d) was allowed to perform in Kallipolis. By contrast, in book 10 Socrates describes himself as "not admitting at all any part of [poetry] that is imitative" (595a). He seems to relate this shift to the fact that the "soul's forms have each been separated out" (595a). In other words, Socrates apparently extends and reformulates his attack on poetry—specifically on the tragedians and Homer (595b)—because now, after the tripartite scheme of book 4 has been developed, he is able to offer a psychologically based critique. It is thus most surprising when his initial argument against poetry has nothing to do with psychology. Instead, it is based on a metaphysical scheme, which apparently refers to the introduction of the Ideas or Forms in book 6 and which condemns not just poetry in particular but imitation in general. This metaphysical argument, however, is formulated in strikingly different, even contradictory, terms from those used in the earlier books.

Socrates begins by describing three kinds of couches. One, the Form of the couch, "is in nature" and is produced by god; a second, the particular couch made from wood, is produced by a carpenter; the third, say a painting, is an imitation of the carpenter's couch. Imitation in general is thereby castigated for being "at the third generation from nature" (597e) and thus "far from the truth" (598b). This is quite strange because, first of all, despite invoking at the outset what

he calls his "customary procedure" of setting down "some one particular Form for each of the particular 'manys' to which we apply the
same name" (596a), what Socrates presents in book 10 is radically
different from anything else he has said in the *Republic*. Strictly fol-
lowed, this "procedure" would generate not only the Form of the
couch but also Forms of houses, onions, and ants. In other words, it
would duplicate the entire world of namable objects. In book 6, however, as Alexander Nehamas (1999) and others have pointed out,
Forms are restricted to a limited set not of objects, things, or artifacts
but of qualities such as beauty, justice, courage, and good. Second, the
introduction of a productive god deviates sharply from any notion of
the divine found elsewhere in the *Republic* (see Cherniss 1932).
Third, in order to model their products on the Form of the couch, car-
penters would presumably require knowledge of that Form. But in
Kallipolis, surely, such knowledge is available only to philosophers,
not to members of the working class.[10]

Charles Griswold (1981) offers a useful interpretation of this passage. He suggests that the metaphysical argument is "intentionally
ironic" (139). He elaborates the points I made in the preceding para-
graph as follows:

(1) The argument seems to refer to the Ideas in Republic 6. A major
problem is that "Socrates' previous discussion of the Ideas in *Republic* 5–7 not only failed to refer to artifacts, but also omitted
reference to Ideas of things" (135).

(2) The one-over-many procedure "leads to the setting down of Ideas
for virtually everything" (136). As mentioned, this move would
simply reproduce the sensible world as an intelligible one, and
support for it cannot be found in book 6.

(3) God appears as creator of Ideas. There is no mention of a productive god anywhere else in the dialogue.

(4) Craftsmen "see" the Ideas as they produce their artifacts. Earlier,
it seemed that only philosophers could do so, but "it seems that
now anyone (except) imitators can simply see the Ideas with no
difficulty" (145)

Griswold characterizes this entire scheme as not merely "strange"
but "unintelligible" (1981, 146). Consider, for example, the relation-

10. One extreme and thoroughly unsatisfying way of explaining such anomalies is
to argue that book 10 was written later than the rest of the dialogue and added after-
ward as some sort of appendix. See, for example, Else 1972.

ship between the craftsman and the Ideas. What sort of Idea, Griswold asks, would a craftsman see when building a particular bed? "Perhaps he would see a blueprint for a bed." But "what language would [such a blueprint] be written in? What materials would it recommend? Are there not many perfect kinds of beds, depending on the given contingent situation?" (145). In other words, this aspect of the tripartite scheme is difficult to take seriously. Why, then, would Socrates assert it here?

Griswold's proposal is ingenious. Consider his explanation of Socrates' introduction of a productive, creative god. Such a view would clearly be prohibited by the censorship of the myths outlined in books 2–3. In Kallipolis, god must be depicted as simple and arithmetical: that is, as never "departing from his own idea" (381c). Such a god is the cause not of "everything" but only of "things that are in a good way" (379b). Such a god, who is utterly unlike the Olympians found in the Homeric poems, could not make a Form of a lowly couch. The disparity between the officially sanctioned theology of book 2 and the productive god of book 10 leads Griswold to conclude that "Socrates' statements in book 10 about God . . . are in effect equivalent to the assertions of the uncensored poets" (1981, 142). In other words, the metaphysical scheme—God-forms, craftsmen-artifacts, imitators-imitations—is not a reflection of Plato's views but "a representation of the poet's conception of the Whole" (146).

Griswold explains the notion of Forms of artifacts similarly. On its own terms this notion is deeply problematic because the list of artifacts is constantly changing. Presumably, there was no Idea of the computer in 400 B.C.E., but there is one now. If so, then the Forms are not eternal. Indeed, the notion of a god endlessly creating new Forms of new artifacts puts excessive emphasis on production or genesis. "The imitator or poet concerns himself solely with genesis . . . the whole schema of Idea-God, artifact-artisan, imitation-imitator, is shot through with the language of genesis. Idea, artifact, imitation, are all made, and so have all become at one time or another. God, artisan, artist, themselves change at one time or another, and have no stable paradigms for their activity" (1981, 146).

In sum, the poet embraces a Heraclitean world in which there is nothing but generative flux. Consequently, this world view must collapse on itself, for it contains the sorts of self-reference problems that plague the flux and which Socrates spells out in such detail in the *Theaetetus*. As Griswold puts it, "The poetic conception of the

Whole cannot internally sustain itself, because it is unreflexive" (149). With its utter emphasis on production it cannot offer a stable account of itself. It cannot, therefore, be itself. Griswold thus describes the passage as a "caricature of the poet's own vision of the Whole" (1981, 142).

The poet, falling into a whirlpool of his own making, really does not know what he is talking about. More specifically, the poet himself occupies the lowest place in the scheme, at a third remove from truth. Of course, poets would not knowingly locate themselves as beneath the craftsmen, but in the terms of the scheme itself, this is where they belong. They fail, in other words, to reflect on their own lowly status within their own poeticized world view. The "poet does not discuss himself or his poetry within his poem. . . . He in effect excludes himself from his own universe of discourse." The poem "does not seek to know itself" (Griswold 1981, 149).

Even if Griswold's interpretation of the passage is acceptable, it does not explain why, at this juncture of the *Republic*, Plato has Socrates present a reductio ad absurdum of the poet's world view. For this, I return to my initial statement: a crisis has been reached. Books 8 and 9 have shown that philosophy requires poetry in order to give an adequate account of the human soul. But philosophy is not identical to poetry. Hence, there is an urgent need for Socrates to differentiate the two. The difference is disclosed through the metaphysical argument which, as Griswold has it, represents the poetic world view itself. The poets make no gesture toward, have no conception of, anything stable and intelligible. Theirs is a world view of production and flux; hence, it is incapable of making sense of itself.[11] It is a world view with no appreciation for the great lessons of the arithmetical. As a result, the poet does not turn from becoming to being. The philosopher does.

Before elaborating, I turn next to Socrates' psychological argument against poetry. For many commentators, notably Nehamas (1999), this, rather than the altogether peculiar metaphysical argument, is the key to Plato's quarrel with the poets.

Socrates begins by asking Glaucon "on which one of the parts of the human being does [poetry] have the power it has" (602c). (I retain

11. I don't necessarily endorse this view, and I certainly understand that simply stating it is not equivalent to demonstrating it.

Bloom's translation here, although throughout the passage he consistently imports the word "part" [*meros*] which is not found in the Greek—a serious error, although it is quite helpful in smoothing out the English translation.) To clarify his question, he cites an example similar to one he used to explicate the divided line in book 7 (the bigger and smaller fingers at 523e). A stick in the water may look bent, but out of the water it will look straight. This sort of disturbance or "confusion" (*tarachē*: 602c12) is endemic in the soul. In book 7 it was described as the "barbaric bog" (*borboroi barbarikoi*: 533d1) associated with sense perception, with segment C of the line (figure 2). Such confusion is resolved by those best of "helpers," such mathematical *technai* as "measuring, counting, and weighing" (602d). With their aid, the "contrary appearances" (602e5) inherent in sense perception (the stick is curved, the stick is straight; the finger is bigger, the finger is smaller) are stabilized. The stick's length can be precisely measured and its contours described geometrically, as can the effect of water on light. With such mathematical intervention, the conflict of appearances can be stabilized. Such is "the work of calculation" (*tou logistikou*: 602e1).

Since "it is impossible for the same thing to opine [*doxazein*] contraries at the same time [*hama*] about the same things" (602e8–9)—that is, since the PNO is at work—"the part of the soul opining contrary to the measures would not be same as the part that does so in accordance with the measures" (603a). "The part which trusts measure and calculation would be the best part of the soul," and the "part opposed to it would be one of the ordinary things in us" (603a). (Again, *meros* does not appear in the Greek.)

Seeing a stick as both straight and curved manifests what is "ordinary" in us: our sense perceptions. By contrast, when we measure the stick and then "see" it as fixed and stable, we engage in rational activity. Since the two are opposites (one reports a conflict, one does not), they must emanate from or reflect distinct "parts" of the soul.

This psychological scheme is, according to Nehamas (1999) the backbone of the critique of imitation. Simply put, "imitation"—and therefore the real target of this attack, the poetry of Homer and the tragedians (595b)—nourishes what is "ordinary" in the souls of the audience by representing it at work in the characters depicted in the poem. Hence, it is condemned.

For Nehamas, this psychological argument straightforwardly represents Plato's views and harks back to the tripartite psychological

scheme of book 4. He notices, of course, one obvious difference between this argument and the earlier one: in book 10, Socrates speaks
of two different psychological capacities capable of "opining." From
this, Nehamas infers that "we can take Plato to be distinguishing between two aspects of reasoning, both belonging to the rational part of
the soul: the uncritical acceptance of the senses' reports on the one
hand, and reflective judgments about them on the other" (1999, 265).
In book 4, he continues, Socrates only "very roughly" distinguishes
parts of the soul, while in book 10 he "is making a finer distinction
within our rational motives" (265). By contrast, when it comes to the
"irrational" parts of the soul, Nehamas's Plato is actually less clear:
"In this passage Plato seems to oppose reason both to spirit (*thumos*)
and to appetite (*epithumetikon*). . . . Poetry is likely to depict conflicts between reason on the one hand and some lower part of the soul
on the other. Sometimes that lower part is appetite [and] . . . sometimes it is spirit" (267).

In any case, the works of the imitative poets are directed at the "irritable and various character" (605a5) of the soul. For this reason they
"seem to maim the thought [*dianoias:* 595b6] of those who hear
them." Socrates elaborates through an example of a father who has
lost a son. A decent man would "fight the pain and hold out against it
more when he is seen by his peers" (604a); only when alone would he
indulge his grief, because "argument and law tell him to hold out."
Because a psychological version of the PNO is at work—"when a contradictory tendency arises in a human being about the same thing at
the same time [*hama*], we say that there are necessarily two things in
him" (604b)—it can be inferred that the man's soul has two "parts."
The first is rationally compelled to conclude that none of "the
human things are worthy of great seriousness" (604c), and therefore,
one should keep quiet in public over the loss of a beloved son. The
second, the emotional part, is longing to cry. Since "the best part is
willing to follow this calculation" (604d), a decent man keeps quiet.

Socrates describes this "part" as "always nearly equal to itself"
(604e). To use the terminology of the second section of chapter 1, it is
arithmetical or numberlike. Precisely because of its stable and self-
identical nature, it is rarely the subject of poetry. To imagine a good
story about a hero who suffers no emotional distress and does nothing but calculate is difficult. Far more common, and much more en-
tertaining, are representations of the "irritable" (*aganaktētikon:*
604e2) aspect of the soul, which "affords much and varied [*poikilēn:*

604e1] imitation." Good stories move their audiences but only when the characters are emotionally charged and psychologically conflicted. In short, the unity and domination of the rational "part" of the soul are jeopardized by the disruptive force of the emotions, which in turn are precisely the subject of the poet's imitations. On this basis, according to Nehamas, Plato condemns poetry; his "proscription . . . allows of no exceptions" (1999, 251).

Nehamas's reading of the psychological argument against poetry in book 10 is sensible enough. Socrates seems to re-invoke the familiar tools of the PNO and some version of the tripartite division of the soul and then to enter the "old quarrel between philosophy and poetry" (607b5), prepared to battle for the supremacy of reason. But this reading suppresses the genuine complexities, and has no way of explaining the discrepancies, of book 10. For example, why does Socrates in book 3 allow some measure of imitation but in book 10 prohibit all of it? Even though he believes this contradiction "cannot be ultimately eliminated" (1999, 254), Nehamas does think it can be considerably softened. The book 3 allowance of imitation, he argues, is aimed only at children, who can benefit from small doses of carefully regulated poetry, whereas the book 10 blanket condemnation targets adults. "Though children can learn from imitation, the adult inhabitants of the city are not to be exposed to it" (255).

Although this conclusion is effective as a logical solution to the apparent contradiction, it glosses over several difficulties. Who in the city would compose and perform the imitations that the children attend? Who would chaperone them? Wouldn't adults accompany the children to the recitations and performances? At what age does a child become an adult? How would recently turned adults recover from the impact of the stories they heard as children? In sum, Nehamas's proposal makes little sense on a practical level.

So too does Nehamas fail to explain the radical difference between the metaphysical scheme Socrates uses to condemn imitation in book 10 and the terminology he employs in books 6 and 7. He only describes it as "strange," while noting that "little of what Socrates says about the Forms is actually relevant to his definition of imitation" and that, because Plato is ultimately dependent on the psychological argument, he "does not clearly require the dubious one-over-many of 596a ff, or Forms of artifacts, or God as the creator of such Forms" (1999, 257). This may be so, but why then is the metaphysical scheme there?

Finally, Nehamas uncritically substitutes "Plato" for "Socrates" throughout his essay, thereby disregarding the possiblity that Socrates might not, at this particular juncture of the dialogue, straightforwardly represent Plato's views. He treats *Republic* 602c–605c as an independent argument by isolating it from its context within the dialogue as a whole. This last error is disastrous, for Socrates' critique of poetry in book 10 manifestly contradicts his own use of narrative and imitation in books 8 and 9, a portion of the *Republic* that relies heavily on the "irritable and various" aspects of the soul. Characters such as the son of the aristocrat, the timocratic father, the dreaming democrat, and the tyrant are repressed, conflicted, highly emotional, and insanely ambitious; as a result, they are both interesting and uniquely informative. The preceding section of this chapter argued that the move to narrative was critical for the completion of Plato's psychology. By identifying Socrates' comments about poetry in book 10 with Plato's views, Nehamas, like Annas, would be forced to dismiss books 8 and 9 as philosophically insignificant.

In response to Nehamas: although Socrates' psychological argument in book 10 clearly harks back to the tripartite division of the soul in book 4, it does not simply reproduce it. Instead, it reformulates it precisely in order to highlight its inadequacy. Consider the following examples. Plato avoids the word "part" throughout book 10. The language he uses, which Bloom obscures, thereby leaves open the possibility that the soul "acts as a whole." So too does his remark that "the part of the soul opining contrary to the measures would not be the same as the part that does so in accordance with the measures" (603a). In other words, different "parts" of the soul do the same work: they "opine" and hence cannot be conceived of as distinct parts at all. Similarly, Socrates' characterization of poetry as appealing to and nourishing what is "irritable and various" in our souls actually obscures the nature of this supposedly lower "part," which he describes as follows: "And as for sex, and spiritedness, too, and for all the desires, pains, and pleasures in the soul that we say follow all our action, poetic imitation produces similar results in us. For it fosters and waters them when they ought to be dried up [*auchmein*: 606d]." The conjunction of sex, spiritedness, pain, and pleasure blurs the boundaries between them and therefore calls into question the distinct nature of this putative "part."

There is a deeper sense in which the passage just cited shows why the tripartite psychology of book 4 is not, *pace* Nehamas, simply reproduced and affirmed here in book 10 but instead is reiterated in its problematic character. Socrates says that poetry "fosters and waters" our lower parts, which should in fact be dried up and allowed to wither away. But such a psychological regimen is thoroughly at odds with the basic dynamics found in the second and third waves of the *Republic*. For example, being dry is characteristic not of the philosopher—who is far from withered but passionate in his quest for being and stability—but of the oligarch, who is a "squalid" or "dried up" (*auchmēros*: 554a10) sort of man. The oligarch is petrified by his love of money, none of which he can bring himself to spend or enjoy. He lives in a tiny world governed by a dry and lifeless ledger sheet. By contrast, philosophers are described through the "hydraulic model" of desire (see Kahn 1987, 97): their desires "have flowed toward learning" (485d). As opposed to a static, dry model of a tripartite soul, human Eros is a fluid, boundary-breaking swelling. Philosophy, properly understood, is wet precisely because it aspires to the static, dry immobility of the Forms.

In this light, reconsider the initial remarks that Socrates makes about imitation: "The tragic poets and all the other imitators . . . seem to maim the thought of those who hear them and do not have knowledge of how they really are as a remedy [*pharmakon*: 595b6]." In other words, poetry dis-eases us, makes us unhealthy and in need of medicine. Similarly, he also says that imitation "is not comrade and friend for any healthy or true purpose" (603b1–2). "Healthy" and "true" are precisely the two adjectives Socrates used to describe the city of pigs (372e5–6), the dry and peaceful city free from conflict, government, philosophy, courtesans, and perfumes: that is, the strictly arithmetical, non-erotic city in which Glaucon, spokesman for the indefinite expansion of desire, refuses to live. In short, it is never simply the case in the *Republic*, as the example of Theages (496b–c) is meant to show, that illness is bad and health unequivocally good. Instead, what is ultimately at issue and in need of accurate depiction is the process by which the "feverish" soul aims for a cure.

At one point Socrates asks, "Is a human being of one mind" [*homonoētikôs*: 603c10]? He does so in order to set the stage for his description of the decisive effect of imitative poetry on the human soul: it disrupts; it threatens the psychological unity and comfort of its audience by representing the compelling spectacle of psychological conflict. Again, it "fosters and waters" what is diverse, multifold, conflicted, variegated, complex in the human soul. By contrast, reason understood as calculation both is and treats what is "nearly equal to itself" (604e): that is, the arithmetical. The goal of reason is to transcend the "barbaric bog," the diverse disturbances of the lower part, and ascend to being. The soul aspires to be of one mind, to attain stability and timelessness. Consequently, it is itself *poikilē*, for it contains within itself both a variety of desires and a longing for uniformity. It is erotic and therefore necessarily diverse, but (at least in the person of the philosopher) it desires arithmetical simplicity. It is a wet soul trying to dry out. Both aspects of the human condition must be included in an adequate psychology.

To summarize this line of thought: the psychologically based critique of imitative poetry found in book 10, which Nehamas uncritically ascribes to Plato himself, would be valid only from the perpsective of a divine being capable of apprehending the rational structure of the whole in a glance. But philosophers are human beings animated by the tyrant Eros. Impelled by awareness of their own becoming, they long for being and are thus continually splitting themselves apart.

The psychological critique of poetry in book 10 redeploys, to some extent, the strategy Socrates used in book 4: namely, the imposition of the arithmetical upon the human soul. Here in book 10, however, after the massive developments of books 5–9, the tripartite scheme must itself be read as exaggerated, one-sided, inadequate, and at odds with the *Republic* itself. Yes, Socrates re-invokes the PNO and decries poetry for acting on the lower "part" of the soul. But no, this bit of argument cannot simply be ascribed to Plato as his final view. Instead, it must be understood as a moment in the dialogue. A crisis has developed. Because of Socrates' own use of stories in books 8 and 9, poetry threatens to overwhelm the conception of philosophy being dialectically developed in the *Republic*. To establish some sort of stable bulwark against this intrusion, Socrates re-invokes the arithmetical version of his psychology, albeit in modified and provocative terms. It is vital to remember that the earlier stages of the dialogue, particularly the first wave with its exaggerated sense of the one-one, has never been junked by Plato. Its value is retained. In book 10 the

poet needs to be hit with a tripartite conception of soul and a reminder of the role the PNO plays in human life.

As great as, or even greater than, the question "What is the Idea of
the Good?" or "How does 'Plato's theory of Ideas' really work?" is
this one: "Why does Socrates return to the theme of poetry in book
10 and then recast his critique in such peculiar terms?" Even more
pointed: "Why does Socrates, just after offering what appears to be a
scathing indictment of poetry, close the *Republic* with a story, a
poem, of his own—the myth of Er?"

Before actually telling his story, Socrates begins this final scene
with a *logos* that seems designed to secure the basic presupposition of
the myth. He asks, "Haven't you perceived that our soul is immortal
and is never destroyed?" (608d). He then goes on to "prove" this perception with the following (paraphrased) argument:

(1) If A destroys or corrupts B, A is bad.
(2) Every B has some bad A which is "naturally connected" (609a) to
    it.
(3) If there is some B which is made bad by its A but cannot be de-
    stroyed by its A, then B is indestructible.
(4) The soul has several As that are naturally connected to it and
    make it bad: for example, injustice and licentiousness (609c).
(5) The soul's As do not destroy it.
(6) Therefore, the soul is immortal.

The argument might well be question-begging, for by identifying
the "bads" of the soul as injustice and the like, rather than disease or
old age, it assumes from the outset that the soul is independent of the
body. If this argument does not beg the question, the next surely does:

(a) No X can be destroyed by "an alien evil" (610a).
(b) The badness of the body is an evil alien to the soul.
(c) Therefore, the soul cannot be destroyed by the destruction of the
    body.

Socrates summarizes the conclusions of both arguments thus:
"Since [the soul] is not destroyed by a single evil—either its own or an
alien—it's plainly necessary that it be always and, if it be always, that
it be immortal" (611a). Of course, Socrates has in no way proved that
the body is alien to the soul. Furthermore, even if the arguments are

counted as valid (e.g., by conceiving of earlier books of the dialogue as supporting evidence for them), they would fail to secure anything informative about the nature of such immortality. The myth of Er clearly presupposes "personal immortality," a state of the soul after death in which the moral being, the "power and intelligence" (*Phaedo*, 70b) of the person, are retained. The arguments sketched above could (at best) just as well indicate some sort of cosmic immortality or the endurance of a life principle. They disclose nothing about what will happen to *us* after *we* die.

More interesting by far than the arguments themselves is what Socrates infers from them. If the soul is immortal, then "there would always be the same souls. For surely they could not become fewer if none is destroyed, nor again more numerous" (611a). If the number of souls were not a constant, then, Socrates concludes (without explaining exactly why), "everything would end up being immortal" (611a). In turn, he takes this to imply that there must be a cyclical form of reincarnation: the same *number* of souls is endlessly recycled.

This small bit of unsatisfying argumentation sets the stage for what follows. First, it bestows upon the passage an arithmetical luster or tone. A fixed number of souls exist in this world. Precisely this mathematical sheen will characterize the entire myth, which is remarkably vivid in its depiction of a highly structured, intelligible cosmic order. Second, just as the unsatisfying quality of the previous arguments suggests, this appearance of arithmetical lucidity turns out to be superficial and unsustainable. It will be compromised, even undermined, by the actual details of the myth.

Er, twelve days after he was killed in battle, returns to life to report "what he saw in the other world" (614a). The first story he tells is that of the "demonic place" (614c) between heaven and earth where the recently dead arrive to be judged. There are two openings in the earth, and two in heaven. If the soul is just, it heads upward to the right; if unjust, left and down. At the same time that the newcomers are departing, others are arriving. From the left-heaven opening, just souls are returning from their visit to the "inconceivable beauty" of the higher realms; from the right-earth opening the unjust are returning to the central demonic place. Each has received a tenfold punishment or reward for the life it led on earth, which is taken to be one hundred years, and so has been traveling for one thousand years. In sum, the moral cosmos seems to be structured with such mathematical precision that Socrates' description can be captured in a flow chart (figure 3).

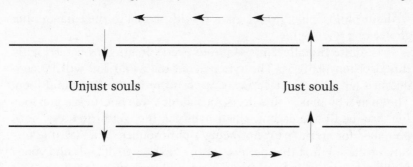

Figure 3

This neat picture is, however, complicated by a crucial detail concerning the "incurables," those whose wrongdoing cannot be treated by the 10-to-1 ratio. Not surprisingly, tyrants are the prime example. A vicious man such as Adriaeus, who not only was a tyrant but also killed his father and did many other unholy deeds, is not permitted to return to the demonic place. Such men "supposed they were ready to go up, but the mouth did not admit them" (615e). Instead, Ardiaeus is grabbed by "fierce men" who bind and flay him and then drag him into Tartarus, where he presumably stays for eternity (616a). He is taken out of the moral loop.

This small deviation from the normal patterns of the flow chart takes on enormous significance later in the myth. After their thousand-year journeys in heaven or under the earth, the souls spend seven days in the demonic place (615b), and then go on a four-day trip to the center of the universe where they glimpse the entirety of its rational structure (more on this below). Here they receive, from Lachesis (one of the Fates), a lot that determines the order in which they will choose their next lives. At this moment of choice, Socrates says, there is "an exchange of evils and goods for most of the souls" (619d). Those who have returned from their punishment below the earth, "because they themselves [have] labored and [have] seen the labor of others, [aren't] in a rush to make their choices" (619d). As a result, presumably, they are sufficiently steeled to make good choices. By contrast, those who return from their thousand years of reward in heaven are seemingly softened and dulled by the pleasures they have experienced and, as a result, are inadvertently primed to make a terrible choice of lives. The first to choose his life is just such a man, "one of those who [has] come from heaven, having lived in an orderly regime in his former life, participating in virtue by habit, without philosophy" (619c). As a result, he makes the catastrophic choice of a tyrant's life.

It is, quite literally, impossible to overestimate how catastrophic this decision really is. The tyrant is an incurable and will be condemned for eternity in Tartarus, never to return to the moral loop. The man who makes this disastrous choice was not, in his previous life, bad; he lived a decent, albeit habitual, life. Yet ultimately, he is punished for eternity for not being a philosopher. The startling feature of the myth is that because of the "exchange of evils and goods for most souls," this fate seems to await almost everyone. If a soul is unjust but not incurable, it will receive a thousand years of punishment below the earth, during which time it will be hardened and thereby made better able to choose a good life the next time around. What if, as seems entirely likely, in the next cycle such a soul chooses a decent but nonphilosophical life? It will be rewarded with a thousand years of pleasure. This millennium of pleasure, however, will presumably stupefy the soul so that, as Er's story has it, it will next be disposed to choose the life of a tyrant, which, in turn, will lead to eternal damnation. Every time this happens—and there is good reason to think it will happen to most souls—the number of souls returning to life will shrink. The arithmetical constancy Socrates seemed to promise in his prefatory *logos* will thus be severely compromised.

The details of the myth are sparse, so there is no way of knowing, for example, whether an unjust but curable soul would actually choose the habitually decent life and then, eleven hundred years later, suffer damnation. Nor is it made clear precisely how the philosopher exempts himself from this pattern. Socrates says only this: "If a man, when he comes to the life here, always philosophizes in a healthy way . . . it's likely on the basis of what is reported from there, that he will not only be happy here but also that he will journey from this world to the other and back again not by the underground, rough road but by the smooth one, through the heavens" (619e). Is the philosopher so self-disciplined as not to become softened by the "inconceivable beauty" of heaven? A thousand years is, after all, a long time. Not all the details of the story are given, but two elements are certain: first, tyrants go to hell; second, only one kind of human being, the philosopher, is somehow exempted from the fate of the tyrant, the self-destructive operation of the moral flow chart. As Socrates made clear in book 6, the majority of human beings cannot "accept or believe that the fair itself, rather than the many fair things . . . is."

Therefore, "it's impossible that a multitude be philosophic" (493e–494a). As a result, most people, all who are not philosophers, will end up in hell.

According to the myth of Er, then, from the perspective of eternity, human beings ultimately face one of only two kinds of lives: philosophy or tyranny.

In addition to its putative moral order, the cosmos as such has a mathematical structure. All souls, except those of the tyrant, are taken to a place where they can "see a straight light, like a column, stretched from above through all of heaven and earth" (615b). From the middle of this column the souls are able to see to the extremes. What they see looks like a spinning wheel with a "great hollow whorl" (615d) in which are contained eight separate whorls—which seem to represent the spheres of the fixed stars, the planets, the sun, and the moon—revolving around a spindle. The eight whorls are organized proportionally according to their breadth: "The circle formed by lip of the first and outermost whorl is the broadest; that of the sixth, second," and so on. Scholars disagree on the ultimate result, but Adam's suggestion (1902, 476) remains reasonable enough. He submits that "the breadth of rims has been taken to mean the distances between the planets" (472) and so arrives at the following scheme:

The whorl of the Fixed Stars (no. 1)
" " " the Sun (no. 7)
" " " the Moon (no. 8)
" " " Venus (no. 6)
" " " Mars (no. 4)
" " " Jupiter (no. 3)
" " " Saturn (no. 2)
" " " Mercury (no. 5)

The picture Adam proposes looks like figure 4.

For my purposes, whether this reading of the symbolism or the diagram is ultimately accurate is not crucial. What matters is that whatever its details, Socrates' story conjures up a picture of a tightly structured cosmos. As Adam puts it, "Plato's representation of the planetary distances in the *Republic* deliberately follows an a priori principle of symmetry and number, selected chiefly in view of the partcular image to which he here assimilates the celestial motions, and suggestive of the balance and equilibrium which ought to prevail in the celestial system" (1902, 474).

A siren sits perched on each of the whorls "uttering a single sound,

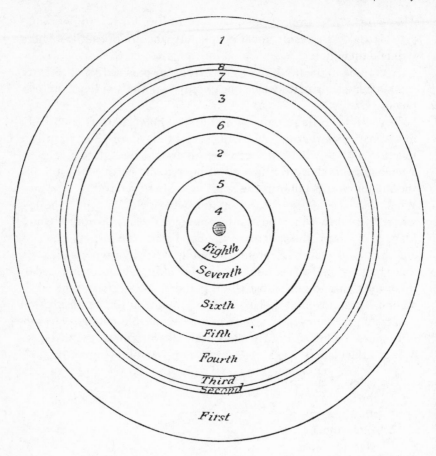

Figure 4

one note" (*mian . . . hena*: 617b6). The three Fates—Lachesis, dispenser of lots; Clotho, the spinner; and Atropos, the inevitable—sing to the harmony produced by the sirens. Reminiscent of the Kallipolean motto "one one" (*heis mian*: 370b6), this element of the story bespeaks the harmony of the spheres, long sought for by astronomers and cosmologists.

The picture is complete, and it seems to be a hopeful one. The world is rational, it tells us, for it is regular in shape, harmonious at its core, and therefore articulable in the purest form of rational language—namely, mathematics. The problem, of course, is that the mode of expressing this message is itself not at all mathematical: it is a story rather than a rational demonstration. There is thus an internal tension in this story of a rational universe, for the telling of the story stands at odds with, or even betrays, the very notion of a rational universe. In other words, if the world were so thoroughly rational, there would be no need for stories. If the myth were true, it would be unnecessary.

Again, the story projects a hopeful vision. But storytelling, from the perspective of the philosopher, the lover of *logos*, is implicit testimony to what is famously described in Plato's "Seventh Letter" as the "weakness of *logos*" (343a1). The paradigmatic Platonic story of a fully intelligible world thus oscillates between hope and despair. Its content projects hope; its form implicitly counsels despair. A myth of this sort, which is found in many dialogues, thus sits on the edge, somewhere between rational intelligibility and mythic assertion. A Platonic myth suggests the possibility that the cosmos can, and therefore should, be demythologized: that is, rendered fully rational.

But the myth of Er does not end here, and its conclusion complicates matters even more. After catching a glimpse of the mathematical luminescence of the cosmos, the souls then receive their lots. To each "it [is] plain what number he [has] drawn" (617e). The lottery numbers determine the order in which the souls choose from the various "patterns" of lives set before them. The number of patterns is "far more than were souls present," and "there were all sorts [*pantodapa*: 618a3]" from which to choose. Because the number of possible lives far exceeds the number of actual ones, no human being can ever fully grasp the complete extent of human possibility. A human being is thus always in a position to be surprised by the way someone else lives, and (a very un-Kallipolean) openness to diversity must therefore be recommended. Indeed, "the whole risk for a human being" lies precisely in being able to respond well to this extraordinary and necessarily unpredictable array of human possibilities. "Each of us must, to the neglect of other studies, above all see to it that he is a seeker and student of that study (*mathēmatos*) by which he might be able to learn and find out who will give him the capacity and knowledge to distinguish the good and the bad life" (618c).

But what study would this be? Would it be the "greatest study" (*megiston mathēma*: 505a2) described in book 6: namely, the Idea of

the Good? It is difficult to see how this would help a soul navigate
through and properly choose among the great number of possible
lives. The Idea of the Good is not, after all, itself a human life. Instead,
it is an object of desire, "what every soul pursues" (505e). Perhaps,
then, studying the Idea of the Good would prepare souls to recognize
a philosopher when they see one. Unfortunately, this option does not
seem to mesh with the final story in the myth, that of Odysseus.

When the souls, after receiving their lottery numbers, must choose
their next life, the habitually virtuous goes first and unwittingly opts
for the life of the tyrant and subsequent eternal damnation. The soul
of Orpheus chooses the life of a swan; Ajax, with the twentieth lot,
the life of a lion. The soul of Odysseus chooses last, and "from memory of its former labors it had recovered from love of honor; it went
around for a long time looking for the life of a private man who minds
his own business; and with effort it found one" (620c).[12]

The finale of Plato's *Republic* is stunningly anti-Kallipolean.
After all, the fundamental objective of the city in speech was to
eliminate the distinction between the private and the political and
to prevent the philosopher from living a private life by forcing him to
return to the cave. Odysseus, by contrast, stays far from the cave, and
though the myth does not explicitly say so, it certainly seems to
privilege his choice of a private life. Odysseus, Socrates says, would
have made the same choice even had he received the first lot, and his
is the only soul to be described as "delighted" (620d) with its choice.
But what prepared Odysseus to make such an unusual and seemingly
excellent choice? No doubt his travels, his labors, his vast experience
with a wide variety of human beings acquainted him well with the
diversity of human possibilites. He had not, presumably, studied
arithmetic or geometry or the harmony of the spheres. Instead, he
was open to adventure and, as a result, opted for a private life. This
choice echoes that of the philosopher who, in the "real" world of actual cities, "keeps quiet and minds his own business" (496d)—that
is, lives a private life.

The myth's conclusion articulates a precarious blend of determi-
nacy and freedom in human life. Once a soul chooses a pattern—and
this is done freely—the choice is rendered "irreversible" by the spin-

12. For a thorough discussion of the relationship between the *Republic* and the
Odyssey, see Howland 1993. Howland 1991 is also excellent at rebutting the usual
chronological interpretation of the dialogues.

ning of Atropos (620e). A human being thus has a character, a soul type, that cannot be escaped. Some beings are "destined" to love money; others, power; and some will long for wisdom. In other words, human beings are determined by the erotic configuration of their souls. We are what we love—and yet destinies are in some sense freely chosen. The myth thus ends with a form of compatibilism which, I propose, reflects for a final time the basic tension at work throughout the *Republic*.

From the very first scene when Polemarchus asks Socrates to count "how many of us there are" (327c), the arithmetical, representing the lure of clarity and being, has been a basic thread in the dialogue. The arithmetical is unmistakably good. It is powerful, informative, and inspiring as it turns the human soul around from becoming to being. Ever present as a disruptive twin, and equally forceful, is Eros the tyrant. Threatening to wreck the most careful calculations and destroy the best-laid plans, Eros—as old Cephalus, quoting Sophocles, tells the reader early on—is "a sort of frenzied and savage master" (329c). It drives us crazy, forces us to aim too high.

Immediately after castigating poetry, Socrates tells a story of an arithmetical cosmos but tells it in an utterly nonarithmetical form— namely, the myth. It is a story in which there is only one genuinely viable option for human beings: the life of the philosopher. And yet, who really is the philosopher? Is he the one who contemplates the harmony of the spheres and the dry wonder of the Forms? Or is he more like Odysseus, fluent in the ways of the human world and primed for adventure? Socrates, of course, incorporates both. He is the man thrilled by the novelty of a "torch race on horseback for the goddess" (328a). (And as previously noted, of course, passing the torch is a long-standing image for sexual reproduction.) He is also the man who proffers the divided line, who sketches a curriculum entirely based on mathematics, who tells the story of Er, the story of a cosmos proportionally arranged and thus fully intelligible. He is the dialectical character of the *Republic*.

Philosophers refuse to accept the poetical world view in which gods make Ideas, craftsmen make artifacts, and painters draw pictures. They refuse to accept, in other words, a world "shot through" with genesis, with production, making, the endless appearance and disappearance of things coming-into-being and passing away. For them, there is more; there is stability and intelligibility, tokened best by the "lowly business of the one, two and three." Turned around and inspired by their awareness of the beauty and instructiveness of the arithmetical, philosophers ask what-is-it questions, push hard beyond the particulars, and long for the universal. This is where their Eros takes them; this is what breaks them in two, making them residents of this world and that, orienting them to both here and there. There is a basic conflict in the soul of a philosopher. The tyrant Eros drives hard, breaking the bonds, demanding attention.

Although they are not poets, philosophers must tell stories. There is—indeed, there must be—room within the philosophical *logos* for *muthos*, as Socrates himself suggests with the remarkably conciliatory comments he makes about poetry:

> If poetry directed to pleasure and imitation have any argument to give showing that they should be in a city with good laws, we should be delighted to receive them back from exile, since we are aware that we ourselves are charmed by them. (607c)
>
> But as long as [poetry] is not able to make its apology, when we listen to it, we'll chant this argument we are making to ourselves as a countercharm, taking care against falling back again into this love [*erōta*], which is childish and belongs to the many. (608a)

Those passages manifest a twin tension. First, Socrates declares that a poetry capable of giving arguments as to why it is beneficial, a poetry capable of defending itself, is acceptable. Such a self-justifying form of poetry is, however, oxymoronic, for if the poet were able to make arguments, he would be a philosopher. Indeed, as Griswold (1981) argues, the poet does not reflect on the nature of his world view and has no concern for the problems of self-reference. The poet tells stories, stitches together his tales, and does not offer arguments. Second, note in the second passage the peculiar phrase "chant this argument" (608a3). What sort of argument needs to be chanted? One who has an argument needs only to articulate it in order to muster its logical force. What place does chanting have in the rational enterprise?

The sum total of these oddities, these self-negating features of both a philosophical poetry and a poetic philosophy, lead to a conception of philosophy as including within it a poetical moment. There is justification, for example, of the stories of books 8 and 9. They are required if one is to articulate fully the temporal experiences of the human soul. A psychological narrative is needed if one is to do full justice to inflections of the human soul. Ultimately, what the myth of Er provides is not a serious articulation of the moral structure of the cosmos—which in the story is unbearably grim and possibly self-annihilating—or of the physical or harmonic structure of the spheres. Instead, like the *Republic* itself, the myth is a psychology, a *logos* of the human psyche. It is a psychological narrative, a story that expresses the human desire for stability and intelligibilty, as well as the human reality of passage through time, diversity, free travel, motion, chaos of chatter, and Odyssean flexibility. It seems to offer counsel (utterly at odds with the message of Kallipolis itself) to lead a private life, far from the uproar of the city. Concentrate on yourself, on the question "What does it mean to be a human being?" The answer cannot be given simply through mathematical formulas or only by staring at the heavens. It requires wandering, familiarity with human paradigms. It requires freedom and diversity and so is "probably" best found in a democracy.

Socrates' poem encourages its own annihilation. In so doing, it is protreptic; it urges its audience to become philosophers. It is a story that bespeaks the arithmetical nature of the cosmos but whose form denies the primacy of the arithmetical. Such, however, is the very character of the *Republic* as a whole. In it there is a character, Socrates, who regularly argues for the goodness, the value, the benefit of *arithmos*. But it is a disastrous mistake to isolate any of these argumentative bits and straightforwardly attribute them to Plato. For at other moments, the storyteller—and never forget that Socrates, like Odysseus among the Phaiakians, is himself narrating the entire *Republic* to an unnamed listener—shifts gears, tells stories and myths, draws images, and makes predictions. No single bit of the dialogue, then, should be isolated and treated as a whole. Similarly, the whole should not be a read as a single argument guided by the norm of logical consistency. Instead, it is a dialectical drama, a dialogue, a conversation that twists and turns, develops, and at times revises what was earlier said. In its totality it gives voice to the truth about the human soul.

The Meaning of "Dialectical"

I. THE TECHNICAL MEANING OF "DIALECTIC"

The two basic senses of "dialectic" active in the Platonic dialogues roughly correspond to the Greek words *dialektikē* and *dialegesthai*. This correspondence can be no better than rough, simply because Plato "has no fixed terminology" (Adam 1902, 141). Nonetheless, the distinction is useful, especially in thinking about the *Republic*.

Consider *dialektikē*. As John Lyons has shown, its suffix implies technical knowledge: "The form in *-ikē* may be used indifferently with or without *technē* and in either case it will be picked up by *technē* with equal readiness" (1967, 143). In general, *-ikē* is used to turn an adjective, which itself is derived from a noun, into the name of a specific *technē*. An example: *hippos* means "horse"; *hippikos* then means "having to do with horses"; and *hippikē* means "the *technē* of horsemanship." The pattern with "dialectic" is the same. The noun is *dialektos*, "discourse, discussion, debate, dialect, or language." *Dialektikos* then means "skilled in language or argument," and *dialektikē* names the *technē*.

More important than the suffix, however, is the origin of the word. It is derived from *dialegesthai*, "to converse, to discuss, to argue." With this a potential ambiguity opens up immediately. "Converse" and "discuss" suggest ordinary linguistic activity. You and I might have a casual conversation about taxes while waiting for the bus. If we are both trained economists, however, we might argue against each other in a formal and public debate on tax policy. The latter could well be governed by a referee, bound by time limits and explicitly formulated rules. Indeed, the very word "argue" implies the potential of becoming formal or technical: that is, of becoming logic. For many scholars, "dialectic" connotes just such technical knowledge. Robinson says that "dialectic is the technical aspect of philosophy" (1984, 71); Kahn describes it as "the technical heartland of Platonic philosophy" (1996, 292).

Unfortunately, it is impossible to determine exactly what this technical aspect is, for Plato's explicit descriptions of it are scattered throughout the corpus and vary considerably. The following four examples, each of which I discuss in an extremely cursory manner, are intended only to remind the reader of this difficulty.

(1) Near the end of the *Phaedrus*, Socrates says that dialectic consists of two prongs: the collection of many scattered particulars "into one idea" (265d), and the division of the collected ideas "according to forms." The latter procedure is described via the metaphor of a butcher: the division should take place along the "natural joints" (265a) of things. Division and collection conceived together are the province of the "dialectical men" (*dialektikous*: 266c).

This passage cannot yield a precise formulation of a method for two reasons. First, it is simply too sparse. Yes, dialectic involves division and collection, but these words are hardly self-explanatory. What is collected? Particulars? What sort of particulars? What is divided? Concepts? Universals? Ideas? Dialectic seems to be a conceptual method for unifying particulars into a form, then dividing forms for the purpose of classification and definition. Is it, then, as Griswold thinks (1986, 185), a "way of organizing what one already knows or thinks one knows," rather than a method of discovery? If so, is it so innocuous as to be philosophically uninformative?

A second obstacle in reading this passage is that the explicit statement about dialectic does not correspond to Socrates' actual procedures in the *Phaedrus*, even though he himself says that he may have stumbled on just these two "forms" of discourse (division and collection) in the dialogue he has just completed. First, he says, he brought together the various particulars of Love, and thereby clarified and stabilized the discussion of it. Second, he divided the various kinds of madness (265d–e). But as Griswold (1986) has shown, a retrospective examination of the *Phaedrus* hardly yields a clear example of dialectic. As he puts it, the "rule-governed procedure" of division and collection described at 265–66 is "artificially simplified" and thus "distorts the underlying complexity" of the dialogue itself. In other words, "the theory of method and the practice of dialogue in the *Phaedrus* do not mesh" (1986, 175, 179). After all, the previous conversation in the *Phaedrus*, which Socrates describes as "playful" and riddled by "chance" (265d), consists of a wide variety of divisions, collections, arguments, myths, assertions, and other forms of discourse. By contrast, the "dialectical men" are supposedly able to eliminate these conversational twists and turns by some sort of technical method of conceptual reduction.

In sum, although the passage does sketch the outlines of a technical version of dialectic, it is skeletal, and the dialogue itself does not instantiate it. However alluring the description may be, it therefore pales in comparison with the actual conversations taking place in the dialogue. Hence, for Griswold, a basic purpose of the *Phaedrus* is not to further the project of technical dialectic but to "point out the limitations of techne" (1986, 179) and the philosophical superiority of *dialegesthai*. (See Griswold 1982 for an elaboration.) Whether he is right, as I believe he is (see Roochnik 1996), or wrong, it is undeniable that the *Phaedrus* cannot yield a precise account of dialectic.

(2) The most sustained examples of the actual practice of dialectic conceived as division come from the *Sophist* and the *Statesman*. The Eleatic Stranger, who has replaced Socrates as the main speaker, performs numerous divisions, commencing in the *Sophist* with the "fisherman." He begins with a genus, namely *technē*, which he then divides into two: the productive and the acquisitive (219c). Proceeding along the acquisitive branch, under which he classifies hunting, he eventually ends up with the fisherman as one who hunts water animals, using barbs (221b).

After this sample, the Stranger constructs the various divisions of the sophist. At first blush, these may seem authoritative and quite technical, but the appearance is deceiving. Some divisions conflict with one another (e.g., the sophist is classified as a practitioner of both the acquisitive [221d] and the productive *technē* [265a]). Each conceptual cut is supposed to be binary, but this procedure often becomes strained and hardly seems to be the work of a butcher finding natural joints. For example, a cut is made between the hunting of land animals and that of swimming animals (220a). But what happened to flying animals? Indeed, as Rosen (1983) has masterfully shown, the divisions are regularly riddled with gaps, obscured by inaccurate summaries, and clouded in various other ways; they are hardly the work of a technically precise method. Consequently, even if dialectic could be identified with division, it would be impossible to determine exactly what this identification means on the basis of what the Stranger actually does.

Perhaps, then, one should turn to the Stranger's explicit description of dialectic.

> Shall we not say that division by kinds, and not supposing that the same form is other, or one that is other is the same, belongs to dialectical knowledge [*dialektikēs epistēmēs*]? ... Therefore the man who is able to do this sees that one idea has been entirely extended through many, with each one of them lying apart, and that many forms differing from one another are embraced by one, and again of one form having been united by many wholes into one, and of many forms having been entirely distinguished. This is the knowledge and ability to distinguish by kinds how each is able to participate and how not.... But you surely, I believe, will not grant dialectic [*to dialektikon*] to anyone except the man who philosophizes purely and justly. (253d–e)

This passage is notoriously obscure and its translation problematic. Stenzel found in it confirmation of his notion of dialectic as "the division of concepts" into a pyramidlike structure culminating in an "atomic form": that is, an indivisible object (1964, 90). Gomez-Lobo offered a comprehensive critique of Stenzel's reading (as well as a painstaking analysis of the translation), arguing that in fact the passage "does not describe Division" at all; instead, "it anticipates the comparison of Being and Not-Being with other Forms" (1977, 47).

Engaging in this dispute means entering into the tortuous world of the "late" Plato, and this I cannot do here. (I would mention one point, however: early in the dialogue the Stranger describes his method of division as being value-neutral; it cannot, for example, distinguish between a general and a louse-catcher [227b]. By contrast, the passage cited above attributes purity and justice to the true practitioner of dialectic.) I note only the obvious: the Stranger's explicit description of technical dialectic cannot easily be attributed to his own divisions. It itself, then, is either nontechnical (i.e., imprecise) or a sketch of the sort of technical enterprise projected later in the dialogue. Whatever it is, it is not readily available.

There seems to be an explicit description of dialectic as the "method of dividing by forms" (286d) in the *Statesman*, as well. Here the "dialecticians" (*dialektikōterous*) are said to be better able to "discover through reason [*logos*] the nature of beings" (287a). But once again, the passage is sparse as well as impossible to reconcile with what has actually transpired in the dialogue itself (although it is clear that dialectic here is not merely "a way of organizing what one already knows or thinks"). For example, the Stranger engages in "division without bisection," to quote Dorter (1994, 209), who offers an excellent commentary. There is a long and mighty strange myth (267c–274d) and an extended excursus on the mean (283b–287b). In other words, the *Statesman*, like all of Plato's dialogues, exhibits a wide variety of *logoi* that can hardly be accounted for by the single notion of dialectic as division. If the actual practices in the dialogue do not offer a conception of dialectic, and the explicit description is itself unclear, a technical meaning is impossible to elicit.

(3) Another statement about dialectic comes from the *Philebus*.

There certainly is no more beautiful road than that whose lover I always am, although it has often deserted me, leaving me alone and perplexed. . . . There is in every case one idea of everything. . . . Assuming that there is in each case one idea, we must search for it. And if we get a grasp of this, after one we must look next for two, if there be two, and if not, for three or some other number; and similarly again for each one of these things, until someone can see not only that the original one is one and many and unlimited, but just how many it is. . . . This is what distinguishes the dialectical [*dialektikōs*] and the disputatious methods of discussion. (*Philebus* 16b–e)

Dialectic is a "road," the source of all the *technai*, a gift of the gods to men, and what distinguishes the "dialectical" from the "eristic" men (17a): that is, those who merely argue. The key in this obscure passage seems to be some sort of "eidetic counting." At the outset there are the one and the many, the limited and the unlimited. In every subsequent case there is one idea and then a search for a second and a third. The ultimate conceptual goal is to see the original unit as one and to be able to cut it into the proper number of eidetic units. This passage, along with some from the *Republic*, seems to provide the strongest support for the Aristotelian story about Plato's "eidetic numbers," a story which, even though alluded to here, is never explicitly recounted in the dialogues themselves.

(4) As in the *Philebus*, the statements about dialectic in the *Republic* take their bearings from mathematics, specifically from the role of hypotheses as expressed via the divided line. It is, seemingly,

some sort of metamathematical reflection that leads to knowledge of the forms. It is a philosophical method of attaining the truth about being which makes no reference whatsoever to sensible items. Socrates is deliberately quiet about the details, apparently because his interlocutors cannot understand them. I cite and discuss these passages from the *Republic* in the third section of this appendix. For the moment, I rely on the following comment by Ferrari, which I believe is accurate.

> About dialectic Plato [in the *Republic*] is deliberately cagey. It is or involves philosophic disputation, as befits its etymological connection with the Greek word for "conversation" (534d, 539b–d); it takes a global unifying view of its topic (537c); it aims to discover the definition of things, and thereby the unchanging principles of all that exists—the "forms"—arriving finally at an understanding of the ultimate principle, the form of the good (511b–c, 532a–b, 533b). But we are not told how it achieves this feat, and scholars dispute whether dialectical activity is some kind of meta-mathematics, or whether it quite transcends the ground that mathematics has prepared. (Ferrari 2000, xxx)

As even this painfully brief review suggests, a series of (almost certainly) irremediable controversies arises when it comes to the technical sense of dialectic in Plato's dialogues. Even if the explicit descriptions of dialectic as division were to cohere with the actual practices of the Stranger in the *Sophist* and the *Statesman*, how would they jibe with the description (or the practices) of division in the *Phaedrus*? What is the relationship between the apparently metamathematical characterization in the *Republic* or *Philebus* and dialectic as conceptual division? How do any of these descriptions cohere with the hypothetical method in the *Phaedo* (75d, 78b, 101e), or the "gymnastic" exercises of the *Parmenides*? (135–36). Finally, how do these highly abstract methodological passages in Plato's "late" dialogues relate to the famous "Socratic method"—that is, the elenctic exposure of contradiction—in the "early" ones?

It is hardly surprising that commentators on the hunt for a technical understanding of dialectic have frequently expressed their frustration. The Kneales begin their *Development of Logic* by (crudely) asserting that as Plato matured, the conception of dialectic in the *Phaedo* and the *Republic* gave way to "the method of division and collection . . . which is discussed in the *Phaedrus* and the *Philebus* and illustrated in the *Sophist* and *Politicus*. The process of division is not clearly explained and remains obscure, but division is evidently the method for seeking definitions by dichotomy of notions beginning with the most general." They conclude that "Plato himself was confused, so that no satisfactory account can ever be given of what he meant by 'dialectic'" (Kneale and Kneale 1984, 9). Not surprisingly, they turn to Aristotle as quickly as they can.

Robinson expresses a somewhat similar sentiment: "The word 'dialectic' had a strong tendency in Plato to mean 'the ideal method, *whatever that may be.*' In so far as it was thus merely an honorific title, Plato applied it at every stage of his life to whatever seemed to him at the moment the most hopeful procedure" (1984, 70).

Despite the difficulties, commentators persist in the hunt for a technical meaning of dialectic. To do so, they must construct elaborate, and therefore highly speculative, chronological interpretations. One of the most delightful remains Gilbert Ryle's: "From the beginning to the end of his writing days," he reports, "Plato's heart was wrapped up in the practice and the propagation of dialectic" (1966, 102). In Ryle's story, the kind of dialectic expressed in the "early" dialogues culminates the "earlier history of dialectic" (110), which began with Zeno and arrived at the *Dissoi Logoi* manual by around 400 B.C.E. It is "a special pattern of disputation, governed by strict rules" (104). As such, it is the ancestor of what is found in Aristotle's *Topics* (albeit in a far more technical form). In fact, says Ryle, "there can be no doubt that what . . . Aristotle calls 'dialectic' is . . . being taught to the young men in the Academy by about the middle 350's" (109). He refers here to the "elenctic question-answer tussles with which in his dialogues Plato credits Socrates" (119). (For dialectic as question-and-answer, see *Republic* 534d and compare with *Cratylus* 390c. For a thorough analysis of the "logic" of the elenchus, see Vlastos 1983, and Benson 2000.)

Ryle argues that as Plato matures, major changes occur. First and foremost, the Theory of Forms takes center stage, and the dialogues cease to represent active question-and-answer debates, becoming more like theoretical treatises. This change is explained by Ryle's most speculative leap. He accounts for "the startling disappearance of the Socratic Method from Plato's dialogues" (1966, 152) by arguing that Plato was legally prohibited from practicing dialectic, whose dangerous political implications are mentioned in the *Republic*: "Don't you notice," Socrates says, "how great is the harm coming from the practice of dialectic these days." The activity of questioning runs the risk of infecting its students "with lawlessness" by undermining parental and political authority (537e–538a). Hence, Ryle argues, it was banned in Athens. In response, Plato turned to a positive Theory of the Forms: "It is legitimate," Ryle claims, "to speculate whether there may not have been a causal connexion between Plato's compulsory divorce from the practice of dialectic and his excogitation of the Theory of Forms." The Forms might represent the ultimate conceptual result of the dialectic that Plato is not allowed to practice. In any case, "Plato's Theory of Forms appears on the scene very quickly after the suppression of his teaching of dialectic to young men and the consequent cessation of his eristic dialogues" (Ryle 1966, 211).

The attempt to chronicle Plato's progress, focusing—as Stenzel (1964), Ryle (1966), Robinson (1984), and Kahn (1996) each do—on the development of his conception of dialectic is a time-honored approach to the dialogues. It represents a search for a technical method and is animated by the hope that philosophy should become as firm as what has become known as science. In this regard, Ryle makes an illuminating remark about the early Plato: "We have to distinguish, as commentators have not always distinguished, between *mere philosophical discussions* [emphasis added] on the one hand, and on the other hand the rule-governed concatenations of questions, answerable by 'yes' or 'no,' which are intended to drive the answerer into self-contradiction. The latter is what should be meant by 'the Socratic method'" (1966, 119) and is the precursor to the more advanced, highly technical conception of dialectic.

Ryle's "mere" is striking, for with it he expresses a fundamental conviction: philosophy should be a technical subject. Therefore, as Plato moves from the disputations of the "early" dialogues to the divisions of the "later," he makes "progress." Apparently, for Ryle, only the technical philosopher is a serious one. This is a view I reject, as I believe Plato himself did.

2. THE NONTECHNICAL MEANING OF "DIALECTIC"

Dialectic as a *technē*, as *dialektikē*, originates in *dialegesthai*. But what sort of relationship obtains between the two? As mentioned, chronologically minded commentators hunt for a continuous development from the early dialogues, where Socrates engages in what (to some) is a logically structured "method" of elenchus, to the later dialogues, where either conceptual division or some sort of metamathematical reflection becomes primary. Because of its plasticity, "dialectic" can be used to denote both stages of Plato's thinking: hence, the title of Robinson's well-known book *Plato's Earlier Dialectic* (whose chapter "Dialectic," especially 61–84, is a useful overview), which argues that "Plato is convinced . . . that dialectic has its beginning only in question-and-answer" (1984, 81). Similarly, Kahn tries to show that there is an "emergence of dialectic" (1996, 292): it is proleptically foreshadowed in the earlier elenctic dialogues and culminates in the later, more technical, ones. Gill, in his "Dialectic and the Dialogue Form in Late Plato," also identifies various features that unify what he takes to be the earlier and later conceptions of dialectic. Most important, in the search for objective knowledge, both earlier and later conception require interlocutors with the "appropriate qualities of character and intellect" (Gill 1996, 185).

The chronologically minded interpreter must construct a plausible conceptual link between the two senses of dialectic: that is, the elenchus and the "new form of dialogue and new method" (Stenzel 1964, 75) alluded to in the later dialogues. I simply assert a proposition I cannot here defend: this task, though laborious, is in fact rather easily accomplished. The Platonic corpus is so rich, so filled with varied threads, that any number of competing but equally plausible views of Plato's progress as a dialectical man can be woven together. The problem with the various stories about "Plato's Progress" is not that they don't make sense; it is that they do. But the specific textual evidence, especially the explicit passages on dialectic itself, is too sparse to offer definitive support to any one of the competing stories. For the purposes of this book it is best, therefore, to remain neutral on the question of whether a technical method of dialectic can be elicited from the corpus read as a whole. Instead of pursuing this question, I turn next to the nontechnical sense of dialectic and to reflections on the *Republic*.

Consider what Gordon says: "Dialectic rests fundamentally on question and answer . . . but dialectic really includes many tropes, behaviors, and ways of being that are embodied by Socrates. Dialectic is the Socratic existential stance" (1999, 20). Gordon's statement is vague, but her work is useful nonethess, for it focuses attention on "dialectic" broadly construed as *dialegesthai*, as "conversation" in all its diverse manifestations. (Note that *dialegesthai* is the infinitive and hence can be used as a noun.) In other words, *pace* Ryle, for Gordon there is no official "Socratic method." There is only Socrates at work conversing with a variety of people in a variety of ways.[1]

Gadamer is well known for making this sort of point.

> If we find in Plato's dialogues and in Socrates' argument all manner of violations of logic—false inferences, the omissions of necessary steps, equivocations, the interchanging of one concept with another—the reasonable hermeneutic assumption on which to proceed is that we are dealing with a discussion. And we ourselves do not conduct our discussions *more geometrico*. Instead we move within the live play of risking assertions, of taking back what we have said, of assuming and rejecting, all the while proceeding on our way to reaching an understanding. (Gadamer 1980, 5)

An example of "dialectic" as "live play," as nontechnical *dialegesthai*, is found in the *Gorgias*. Gorgias wants to give a "display" of his sophistic skills. Socrates, however, is uninterested. Instead he asks, "But would [Gorgias] be willing to discuss [*dialechthēnai*: 447c1] with us?" (Compare *dialegometha* at 449b5.) The ensuing discussion is initially between Socrates and Gorgias, and some of it takes the question-and-answer form (449d–461b). But as McKim argues (1988, 42–45), and as Gordon seconds (1999, 22), "It is not [simply] by logical but psychological means that Socrates aims to persuade his interlocutors, and shame is his psychological tool." Indeed, both Polus and Callicles complain that shaming his opponent is Socrates' basic strategy (461b, 482e). Therefore, what goes on in the conversation between Socrates and Gorgias can be neither adequately described as nor reduced to question-and-answer refutation: that is, logical elenchus. Even if it could, it certainly would fail to account for the remainder of

---

1. See also Gonzalez (1998), who also rejects the notion of "discussing dialectic under the heading of 'methodology' or 'logic'" (2). He usefully focuses instead on what Socrates actually does in the dialogue. His position is quite complicated: dialectic has "the aim of overcoming the limitations of the means it employs"; so, for example, propositions are necessarily ambiguous and arguments are unable "to guarantee perception of the truth" (245). "The dialectician exposes the weaknesses of names, propositions, and images in order then to overcome these limitations in the actual practice of dialectic. The result is an insight that transcends the weaknesses of the means to attain it, but that for this very reason cannot be expressed by these means" (245–46). In short, the knowledge achieved by dialectic is not propositional and "its source must be found in one's own nature or disposition." I don't endorse this position but cite it only to suggest that a broad understanding of dialectic is useful.

the dialogue, which finds Socrates presenting a full-blown conceptual scheme to Polus (462b–466b) in which he asks no questions. Indeed, here he makes a series of assertions, one of which, that rhetoric is not a *technē* (463b), contradicts the basic presupposition of his refutation of Gorgias: namely, that rhetoric is a *technē* (447c). Especially in his conversation with Callicles, Socrates employs a wide variety of argumentative strategies. Although he does engage in standard refutative strategy—for example, by attempting a reductio ad absurdum (489d–491a)—he also tries to shame Callicles by comparing him to a urinating bird (494b), and he tells a myth (523b–526d).

As Gadamer puts it, the "live play" of the conversation does not proceed *more geometrico* (1980, 5), and thus its character cannot be captured by a singular conception of a dialectical or elenctic method. Instead, there is abundant *dialegesthai*, diverse conversations between various kinds of people who react differently to what is said. There is elenchus. For example, from statements to which Gorgias has agreed, Socrates does generate the contradictory propositions that rhetoric does and does not teach justice (460b–d). Still, this is a moment, rather than the essence or the whole, of the dialogue.

Consider *Protagoras* 334e–335b. Socrates complains about the sophist's long speeches; instead of listening to monologues, he wants "to converse" (*dialexesthai*: 335a2). But what does this mean? It means to argue about the unity of the virtues (329d–334c), to interpret a poem by Simonides (339b–347a), and to concoct a scheme about the measuring *technē* (356d). Again, there are strictly elenctic moments of question-and-answer, but the *logoi* are diverse. And they are all embraced under the verb "to converse."[2] Precisely this situation obtains in the *Republic*. Early on, Polemarchus says, "We'll talk" (*dialexometha*: 328a9). This promise is fulfilled in a variety of ways in the *Republic* as a variegated whole. Included among the diversity of *logoi*, and therefore embraced under the more general rubric of *dialegesthai*, is the seemingly technical description of dialectic as metamathematical reflection.

Dialectic in its nontechnical inflection is as difficult to pin down as *dialektikē*, but for an entirely different reason. Precisely because it is informal and constituted by the interlocutors' responses to the par-

2. A few more examples: *Theaetetus* 167e and 161e; *Republic* 328a, 336c, 360a, 515b, and 528a.

ticulars of their conversation, it is necessarily diverse and without a fixed structure. As Griswold puts it, "There is no comprehensive reflection on the meaning of *dialegesthai*" in the dialogues (1982, 116). Nonetheless, a few general observations about it can be ventured.

(1) It requires more than one person: that is, it is dialogical. One can, however, conceive of an internalized dialogue. Indeed, in two similar passages, *Theaetetus* 189e–190a and *Sophist* 263e, thinking itself is described as such a conversation. Still, its basic meaning surely implies what Gill calls a "shared search" (1996, 185).

(2) Because it is dialogical, dialectic is "site-specific." In conversation, I talk to you, and what I say must be appropriate to who you are. As Strauss puts it, Socrates (and in fact the Platonic dialogue itself) "says different things to different people" (1978, 52). In other words, conversation shares two features traditionally associated with rhetoric: it requires an "appropriate" response (*to prepon*) to a particular occasion (*kairos*) constituted by specific individuals, time, and place.[3]

A Platonic dialogue is an imitation of a living conversation. As such, it includes a variety of participants and their unpredictable responses to what is said. Intrinsic to it, therefore, are the presence of particulars and a dimension of contingency.

(3) A structural feature of a conversation is the possibility of interruption. Meno, for example, is one of the most intractable of all interlocutors. After Socrates gives him a model of the sort of answer he is seeking to the question, "What is virtue?"—namely, "Shape is that which always follows color" (*Meno* 75b)—Meno asks, "What is color?" His clear intention is to evade the what-is-it question. He succeeds. Eventually, Socrates yields to Meno's demand (86d) and takes up the issue of the teachability of virtue before determining what it is. Meno's interruptions thereby dictate the course, as well as diminish the quality, of the conversation.

Such moments abound in the dialogues. The slave boy, as well as Anytus, appears abruptly in the *Meno*; Hippocrates awakens Socrates in the *Protagoras*; Theodorus unexpectedly brings the Eleatic Stranger with him in the *Sophist*; and the drunken Alcibiades destroys the orderly progression of speeches in the *Symposium*. As ex-

---

3. For these terms, see Isocrates *Against the Sophists* 13.

plained in the body of this book, Glaucon's dissatisfaction with the "city of pigs" and Polemarchus's aggressive "arrest" of Socrates at the beginning of book 5 are the pivotal transitions of the *Republic*. Again, the inclusion of interruption reaffirms the ineluctable role of contingency and particularity in Plato's dialogues.

To illustrate this point by means of contrast: in the *Theaetetus*, Theodorus is delighted by Socrates' "digression," his description of Thales and the leisure and freedom enjoyed by the philosopher (173a).[4] He enthusiastically responds: "For you have described this very well, that we who are in the chorus of [the philosophers] are not servants of the arguments, but the arguments are our servants" (173c). Theodorus, the mathematician, is captivated by a conception of *logos* which he can thoroughly master. His model, of course, is *technē*. Even if such mastery is attainable in a geometric proof, it is not available in a conversation with another human being who may well interrupt and thereby force the *logos* to take an unexpected turn. This is why, when Theodorus comes to see Socrates on the morning after the *Theaetetus*, he brings with him the Eleatic Stranger, who admits that he does not want to participate in a dialogue. He would rather lecture. If he must converse, he wants a passive interlocutor who will not interrupt him (*Sophist* 217c–d). No wonder Theodorus, and pointedly not Socrates, identifies the Stranger as a great philosopher (216a).

Socrates is radically different from Theodorus or the Stranger. He risks the "live play," the unexpected twists, of a conversation. He is willing, even eager, to be interrupted. When Glaucon and Adeimantus assert themselves in book 2 of the *Republic*, he clearly welcomes their aggressive and intrusive style (367e).

(4) With interruptions come digressions. This is why it is impossible to pinpoint the subject of a Platonic dialogue. (Is the *Charmides* about moderation, or self-knowledge, or knowledge of ignorance, or the unity of the virtues? Is the *Theaetetus* about knowledge or perception or becoming and being? And so on.) Of course, digressions are crucial in the *Republic*.

(5) Digressions may include significant revisions of earlier statements. In the *Protagoras*, for example, Socrates initially said that

---

4. The Thales-like figure described in the "digression" bears little resemblance to Socrates.

virtue is not teachable (319b). By the end of this much-interrupted dialogue, he seems to have reached the opposite conclusion, that virtue can be taught (361d). Revisions may be positive or negative. In the *Meno*, Socrates seems to revise his view that virtue is wisdom (88b) by allowing that "true opinion is in no way a worse guide to correct action than knowledge" (97b). This modification, if it is that, represents a downward turn in the dialogue generated by the base and intransigent Meno. By contrast, the revisions in the *Republic*, sparked by the interruptions of far superior characters, are more productive.

(6) As repeatedly emphasized in the body of this book, earlier moments or stages of a dialogue which are revised and thereby negated are not merely jettisoned; rather, they are preserved in the conversation as a whole. In other words, Plato articulates his views not in a single part of the dialogue but only in the whole. If his purpose were simply to express a set of true propositions—that is, a theory—he would have had no reason to write dialogues. In the *Meno*, for example, Socrates first argues that virtue is knowledge and hence teachable (87d–88d) and then that virtue cannot be taught (89c–89e, 93d–94d). Does Plato therefore simply believe that virtue cannot be taught? No. The right answer to the question is "no and yes." No, it cannot be taught in anything like a standard manner: that is, like a *technē* (the paradigmatic form of teachable knowledge). But yes, it can be taught, if by this one means that virtue is entering into philosophical dialogue itself.

The key example in the *Republic* of dialectical revision is the negation of the tripartite or arithmetical conception of city and soul found in book 4. This negation implies not that the arithmetical conception is simply false but that it is partial. It needs to be revised, but it also needs to be preserved. The arithmetical is theoretically informative and practically useful, especially in dealings with characters like Glaucon. It is not, however, sufficient to account for an erotic, essentially temporal, soul.

The *Republic* is a dialectical ascent. The *logos* of the soul presented in the second and third waves (books 5–7 and 8–10) offers a richer account of what it means to be human than that available in book 4. This progress, however, is neither entirely smooth nor systematic. Indeed, Socrates interrupts himself in book 10. Because he used stories in books 8 and 9 to express his thinking, he is forced to return to the "old quarrel between philosophy and poetry." He has to clarify further what differentiates the two.

The relationship between the "dialectical character" of the *Republic* and what Hegel means by "dialectic" must now be addressed. I begin by noting the most significant difference between the two. Hegelian dialectic is highly technical and meant to attain systematic results. "Knowledge," Hegel says, "is only actual, and can only be expounded, as Science or as system" (1977, 13). By contrast, Platonic *dialegesthai* is informal and infected with particularity and contingency. For precisely this reason, Hegel, a bit like Ryle, criticizes it. (See Griswold 1982, 116–17, for a discussion of Hegel's criticisms of the "Socratic method.") By contrast, he favors the (apparently) technical exercises of the *Parmenides*, describing them as "surely the greatest artistic achievement of the ancient dialectic" (Hegel 1977, 44).

Nonetheless, there are similarities worth mentioning. First, Hegelian dialectic proceeds and ascends by means of negation. Hegelian logic has three "aspects" (*Seiten*): the abstract work of the understanding, which is akin to what I have been calling the "arithmetical"; the dialectical or the negative-rational, the moment of negation; the speculative or the positive-rational, the taking up to a higher level (Hegel 1975, 168). The crux of the conceptual process is what Hegel calls the *Aufhebung*, meaninglessly translated into English by "sublation." The key to Hegel's use of this word is the fact that *Aufheben* has a twofold meaning: "on the one hand it means to preserve, to maintain, and equally it also means to cause to cease, to put an end to. . . . Thus what is sublated is at the same time preserved; it has only lost its immediacy but is not on that account annihilated" (Hegel 1969, 107). No wonder that Hegel chooses the following metaphor to describe this conceptual process:

> The bud disappears in the bursting-forth of the blossom, and one might say that the former is refuted by the latter; similarly, when the fruit appears, the blossom is shown up in its turn as a false manifestation of the plant, and the fruit now emerges as the truth of it instead. These forms are not just distinguished from one another, they also supplant one another as mutually incompatible. Yet at the same time their fluid nature makes them moments of an organic unity in which they not only do not conflict, but in which each is as necessary as the other, and this mutual necessity alone constitutes the life of the whole. (1977, 2)

Dialectical development progresses from abstract, and hence partial, "moments" to more comprehensive ones. As Hegel puts it, "reason is purposive activity" (1977, 12) whose telos is the final "absolute/concrete" (1975, 314): that is, a comprehensive unity of earlier abstract moments, which are necessary for the organic development to take place, as well as their negations and the more complete concepts that ensue. To cite the Hegelian motto, "The true is the whole" (1977, 11) rather than one of its parts: that is, it is quite different from a conclusion derived from premises.

The *Aufhebung* structure of conceptual development is significantly similar to the dialectical character of the *Republic*. The earlier arithmetical stages, governed as they are by the Principle of Non-Opposition (PNO), are negated, but they are not "annihilated." They are preserved, for the arithmetical continues to play a significant role in human thinking, and the PNO never relinquishes its authority over its domain. In this sense, for Plato too, the true is the whole. But to reiterate the fundamental difference: for Hegel, a dialectical development is governed by necessity, and its result—namely, the complete articulation of the whole—is systematic: The "whole is nothing other than the essence consummating itself through its development" (1977, 11). This development is generated by the internal and necessary self-movement of the concept. Therefore, although the Hegelian *Aufhebung*, with its notion of progress from the abstract to the concrete and its commitment to the true as the whole, is useful in articulating the *Republic*'s dialectical character, the differences are more fundamental. The development that is the *Republic* is not an immanently unfolding one, for it is generated by contingent and unexpected interruptions, principally those occurring in books 2 and 5. The "whole" that the dialogue articulates is thus not purely conceptual. The only whole available in the dialogue is the one comprising specific characters and occurring at a particular time and place. Although it offers great insight into the soul and the city, the dialogue is nonetheless an imperfect, hopelessly human enterprise.

To reformulate: the *Republic* does not present a complete account of the truth of the whole. Instead, and especially in books 6 and 7, it articulates the human longing for such truth. In this sense it is a psychology, a *logos* of the soul. Again, the contrast with Hegel could not be more pronounced. As he puts it, "To help bring philosophy closer to the form of Science, to the goal where it can lay aside the title 'love of knowing' and be actual knowing—that is what I have set myself to do" (1977, 3). Plato's *Republic*, by contrast, articulates, imitates, gives voice to just that love.

3. DIALECTIC IN THE *REPUBLIC*

Of the *Republic*'s three most explicit descriptions of dialectic in an apparently technical sense, Kahn notes that in the first and the third, the phrase "the power of dialectic" actually translates *tē tou dialegesthai dunamei* (511b4). He claims that here the verb no longer carries its "ordinary" meaning of "converse" but instead is used as a "semi-technical" term (Kahn 1996, 326).[5] As mentioned at the outset of this appendix, a straightforward mapping of the two conceptions of dialectic onto the two different words is impossible, for Plato does not use a technical vocabulary: that is, a set of terms with stipulated definitions.

Here are the three passages.

> The power of dialectic [makes] the hypotheses not beginnings but really hypotheses—that is, stepping-stones and springboards—in order to reach what is free from hypothesis at the beginning of the whole. When it has grasped this, argument now depends on that which depends on this beginning and in such fashion goes back down again to an end; making no use of anything sensed in any way, but using forms themselves, going through forms to forms, it ends in forms. (511b–c)

> [The five mathematical studies—arithmetic, geometry, solid geometry, stereometry, harmonics—are] a prelude to the song itself.... For surely it's not your opinion that the men who are clever at these things [the five studies] are dialecticians.... [Dialectic] is in the realm of the intelligible ... when a man tries by discussion [*dialegesthai*], by means of argument without the use of any of the senses, to attain to each thing itself that is and doesn't give up before he grasps by intellection itself that which is good itself.... Don't you call this journey dialectic [*dialektikē*]? (531d–532b)

> You would no longer be seeing an image of what we are saying, but rather the truth itself, at least as it looks to me. Whether it is

---

5. Furthermore, as Kahn has shown (1996, 327), *dialektikē* is actually quite rare in the dialogues and "disappears entirely from the pages of Plato after the two instances ... from the *Republic* (534e3, 536d6)."

really so or not can no longer be properly insisted on. But that
there is some such thing to see must be insisted on. Isn't it so? . . .
And that the power of dialectic [*dialegesthai*] alone could reveal it
to a man experienced in the things we just went through. (533a)

These descriptions share two now familiar features: they are stunningly sparse and therefore incapable of definitively yielding a precise
account, and they are somehow dependent on mathematics. Dialectic
is "synoptic" (537c); it gives an account of the entirety of being but
does so only in terms of the Forms (486a, 511b). In the guardians' curriculum it is placed on the "top of the studies, like a coping stone"
(534e), and studied, after ten years of mathematics, for five years
(539e). But what exactly is it? It is impossible to say. Socrates himself
suggests that he is deliberately withholding such information from
his interlocutors because they are incapable of understanding him
(533a). Perhaps this implies that Plato has some sort of secret teaching
he communicates only orally in the Academy. Or perhaps there is no
specifically technical sense of dialectic. Perhaps, like Kallipolis itself,
of which it is a part, the technical sense of dialectic is an arithmetically exaggerated moment of the dialogue as a whole. On the divided
line, for example, the Forms are located above mathematical objects:

The men who work in geometry, calculation, and the like treat as
known the odd and the even, the figures, three forms of angles,
and other things akin to these in each kind of inquiry. These
things they make hypotheses. (510c)

Mathematicians go downward on the line. By contrast, dialectical
thinkers transform hypotheses into stepping-stones and thereby
move upward, ultimately to what is "free from hypothesis at the beginning of the whole" (511b). But what is the relationship between,
say, "the odd and the even" and "the form of the beautiful"? What is
the relationship between qualities such as justice, courage, and so on,
and mathematical properties? Not a word is said. The line, however,
is continuous. Presumably, then, it implies a seamless connection between its segments. What this connection might be, however, is not
explained. Only this can be gleaned: dialectic in its technical sense is
metamathematical. Socrates is thus offering a sketch, a projection, of
philosophical thought. At its pinnacle it is pure: "Using forms themselves, going through forms to forms, it ends in forms." Does this description foreshadow *Sophist* 253d–e or the exercises of the *Par-*

menides? Does it refer to work going on in the Academy? I doubt it, but cannot prove that it does not.

Most readers identify books 6 and 7 as the pinnacle of the dialogue. Only in a limited sense is this true. Dialectic as sketched is a deliberately exaggerated projection of an impossibly purified form of philosophical thought. As such, it is in keeping with the "moment" of which it is a part: namely, the construction of Kallipolis, in which genuine philosophy—which "probably" requires the freedom of a democracy in order to take place—is not possible. By the lights of the *Republic* as a whole, philosophy itself is not a technical, metamathematical discipline. Instead, as this entire book (following the suggestion of Stanley Rosen) is meant to argue, it is a curious and precarious blend of mathematics and poetry. Consequently, those few passages in which dialectic is sketched in books 6 and 7 are embraced within the more comprehensive understanding of dialectic as philosophical conversation.

If Socrates were to "proceed to the song itself" (532d)—that is, actually engage in, rather than merely describe, technical dialectic—Glaucon "would no longer be seeing an image of what we are saying, but rather the truth itself" (533a). Except by using the word "form," which he locates above the "mathematicals" on the divided line, Socrates says next to nothing about what this truth itself is. Nevertheless, he is adamant about one matter: "That there is some such thing to see must be insisted on" (533a). He must insist that even if we do not know what it is, there must be some truth itself to be seen. Even if it is only partially formulated via its relationship to mathematics, the truth itself is the ultimate object of the philosopher's desire and is therefore essential in dialectically articulating the truth of the human soul.

Bibliography

Adam, J. 1902. *The Republic of Plato*. Cambridge.

Annas, J. 1982. *An Introduction to Plato's Republic*. Oxford.

Barber, B. 1996. "Misreading Democracy: Peter Euben and the *Gorgias*." In Euben and Wallach 362–375 1996.

Benson, H. 2000. *Socratic Wisdom*. Oxford.

Bloom, A., trans. 1968. *The Republic of Plato*. New York.

Bobonich, C. 1994. "Akrasia and Agency in Plato's *Laws* and *Republic*." *Archiv für der Geschichte der Philosophie* 76:3–35.

Brown, E. 2000. "Justice and Compulsion for Plato's Philosopher-Rulers." *Ancient Philosophy* 20:1–18.

Burnyeat, M. 1985. "Sphinx without a Riddle." *New York Review of Books*, May 30, 30–36.

Cherniss, H. 1932. "On Plato's *Republic* X 597B." *American Journal of Philology* 53:233–42.

Clay, D. 1988. "Reading the *Republic*." In Griswold 1988, 19–33.

Cooper, J. 1984. "Plato's Theory of Human Motivation." *History of Philosophy Quarterly* 1:3–21.

Crombie, I. 1969. *An Examination of Plato's Doctrines*. London.

Dorter, K. 1994. *Form and Good in Plato's Eleatic Dialogues*. Berkeley, Calif.

Dover, K. 1989. *Greek Homosexuality*. Cambridge.

Else, G. 1972. *The Structure and Date of Book 10*. Heidelberg.

Euben, P. 1996. "Reading Democracy: 'Socratic' Dialogues and the Political Education of Democratic Citizens." In Euben and Wallach 1996, A Euben, J., and J. Wallach. 1996. *Athenian Political Thought and the Reconstruction of American Democracy*. Ithaca, N.Y.

Ferrari, G. 2000. *Plato: The Republic*. Cambridge.

Fine, G. 1978. "Knowledge and Belief in *Republic* V." *Archiv für der Geschichte der Philosophie* 60:121–39.

Gadamer, H. 1976. *Hegel's Dialectic*. New Haven, Conn.

——. 1980. *Dialogue and Dialectic: Eight Hermeneutical Studies on Plato*. New Haven, Conn.

Geertz, K. 2000. "The Geometric Number of Plato: A Philosophical Interpretation." M.A. thesis, Boston University.

Gill, C. 1985. "Plato and the Education of Character." *Archiv für der Geschichte der Philosophie* 67:4–18.

——. 1996. *Form and Argument in Late Plato*. Oxford.

Gomez-Lobo, A. 1977. "Plato's Description of Dialectic in the *Sophist* 253d1–e2." *Phronesis* 20:29–47.

Gonzalez, F. 1998. *Dialectic and Dialogue*. Evanston, Ill.

Gordon, J. 1999. *Turning toward Philosophy: Literary Device and Dramatic Structure in Plato's Dialogues*. State College, Pa.

Griswold, C. 1981. "The Ideas and the Criticism of Poetry in Plato's *Republic*, Book 10." *Journal of the History of Philosophy* 19:135–50.

——. 1982. "Reflections on Dialectic in Plato and Hegel." *International Philosophical Quarterly* 22:115–30.

——. 1986. *Self-Knowledge in Plato's Phaedrus*. New Haven, Conn.

——, ed. 1988. *Platonic Readings; Platonic Writings*. New York.

Hegel, G. 1969. *Hegel's Science of Logic*. Translated by A. Miller. London.

——. 1975. *Enzyklopädie der philosophischen Wissenschaften*. Vol. I. Frankfurt.

——. 1977. *Hegel's Phenomenology of Spirit*. Translated by A. Miller. Oxford.

Howland, J. 1991. "Re-Reading Plato: The Problem of Platonic Chronology." *Phoenix* 45:189–214.

——. 1993. *The Republic: The Odyssey of Philosophy*. New York.

Hyland, D. 1968. "Eros, Epithumia, and Philia in Plato." *Phronesis* 13:32–46.

——. 1989. "Taking the Longer Road: Irony in the *Republic*." *Revue de Metaphysique et Morale* 3.

——. 1995. *Finitude and Transcendence in the Platonic Dialogues*. Albany, N.Y.

Irwin, T. 1977. *Plato's Moral Theory*. Oxford.

Kahn, C. 1987. "Plato's Theory of Desire." *Review of Metaphysics* 41:77–104.

——. 1996. *Plato and the Socratic Dialogue*. Cambridge, Eng.

Keuls, E. 1985. *The Reign of the Phallus*. New York.

Klein, J. 1968. *Greek Mathematical Thought and the Origin of Algebra*. Cambridge, Mass.

——. 1975. *A Commentary on Plato's Meno*. Chapel Hill, N.C.

——. 1977. *Plato's Trilogy*. Chicago.

Klosko, G. 1986. *The Development of Plato's Political Philosophy*. New York.

Kneale, M., and W. Kneale 1984. *The Development of Logic.* Oxford.

Kraut, R., ed. 1997. *Plato's Republic: Critical Essays.* Lanham, Md.

Lachterman, D. 1989. "What Is 'The Good' of Plato's *Republic?*" *St. John's Review* 39:139–71.

Lear, J. 1997. "Inside and Outside the *Republic.*" In Kraut, 1997, 61–94.

Lesses, G. 1987. "The Divided Soul in Plato's *Republic.*" *History of Philosophy Quarterly* 4:147–161.

Lyons, J. 1967. *Structural Semantics: An Analysis of Part of the Vocabulary of Plato.* Oxford.

McKim, R. 1988. "Shame and Truth in Plato's *Gorgias.*" In Griswold 1988, 34–49.

Mara, G. 1997. *Plato's Discursive Democracy.* Albany, N.Y.

Miller, F. 1999. "Plato on the Parts of the Soul." In Van Ophuijsen, 1999, 84–101.

Moline J. 1978 "Plato on the Complexity of the Soul." *Archiv für Geschichte der Philosophie* 60:1–26.

Monoson, S. 2000. *Plato's Democratic Entanglements.* Princeton, N.J.

Nehamas, A. 1975. "Plato on the Imperfection of the Sensible World." *American Philosophical Quarterly* 12:105–17.

——. 1999. *Virtues of Authenticity.* Princeton, N.J.

Nussbaum, M. 1979. "Eleatic Conventionalism and Philolaus on the Conditions of Thought." *Harvard Studies in Classical Philology* 83:63– 108.

Page, C. 1995. "The Truth About Lies in Plato's *Republic.*" *Ancient Philosophy* 11:1–35.

Penner, T. 1990. "Plato and Davidson: Parts of the Soul and Weakness of the Will." *Canadian Journal of Philosophy* 16:35–74.

Ricoeur, P. 1984. *Time and Narrative Vol. 1.* Chicago.

——. 1991. *A Ricoeur Reader.* Toronto.

Robinson, R. 1971. "Plato's Separation of Reason from Desire." *Phronesis* 16:38–48.

——. 1984. *Plato's Earlier Dialectic.* Oxford.

Roochnik, D. 1994. "The Goodness of Arithmos." *American Journal of Philology* 115:285–95.

——. 1996. *Of Art and Wisdom: Plato's Understanding of Techne.* State College, Pa.

Rosen, S. 1983. *Plato's Sophist.* New Haven, Conn.

——. 1988. *The Quarrel between Philosophy and Poetry.* New York.

Ryle, G. 1966. *Plato's Progress.* Cambridge, Eng.

Sachs, D. 1997. "A Fallacy in Plato's *Republic.*" In Kraut 1997.

Samons, L. 2001. "Democracy, Empire, and the Search for the Athenian Character." *Arion* 23:128–57.

Saxonhouse, A. 1996. *Athenian Democracy: Modern Mythmakers and Ancient Theorists*. South Bend, Ind.

——. 1997. "The Philosopher and the Female." In Kraut, 1997, 95–114.

Scott, D. 2000. "Metaphysics and the Defense of Justice in the *Republic*." *Proceedings of the Boston Area Colloquium in Ancient Philosophy* 20:1–20.

Smith, N. 1997. "How the Prisoners in Plato's Cave Are 'Like Us.'" *Proceedings of the Boston Area Colloquium in Ancient Philosophy* 17:187–205.

Stalley, R. 1975. "Plato's Argument for the Division of the Reasoning and Appetitive Elements in the Soul." *Phronesis* 20:110–28.

Ste. Croix, G. E. M. de. 1981. *Class Struggle in the Ancient Greek World*. Ithaca.

Stenzel, J. 1964. *Plato's Method of Dialectic*. New York.

Strauss, L. 1978. *The City and Man*. Chicago.

Szlezák, T. 1976. "Unsterblichkeit und Trichotomie der Seele im zehnten Buch der Politeia." *Phronesis* 21:31–58.

Van Ophuijsen, J., ed. 1999. *Plato and Platonism*. Washington, D.C.

Vlastos, G. 1971. *Plato: Ethics, Politics, and Philosophy of Art and Religion*. New York.

——. 1983. "The Socratic Elenchus." *Oxford Studies in Ancient Philosophy* 1:27–58.1–37

——. 1991. *Socrates: Ironist and Moral Philosopher*. Ithaca, N.Y.

Wedberg, A. 1955. *Plato's Philosophy of Mathematics*. Stockholm.

Whitehead, A. 1971. *The Philosophy of Alfred North Whitehead*. Lasalle.

Williams, B. "The Analogy of City and Soul in Plato's *Republic*," in Kraut, 1997, 49–60.

Wittgenstein, L. 1965. *The Blue and Brown Books*. New York.

Index

Adam, J., 13, 125–26, 133
Adeimantus, 3, 4, 6, 10, 11, 29, 50, 55–57, 70–71, 103
Adriaeus, 123
Akrasia ("weakness of the will"), 13, 104
Annas, J., 13–16, 18, 20, 26, 28, 94, 97–98, 110
Apollo, 43
Apology (of Plato), 83
Aristocracy, 78
Aristotle, 61, 108, 139
Arithmos ("number"), 21, 31, 33–34, 37–39, 68, 76, 109, 131
Aufhebung ("sublation"), 5–6, 147–48

Becoming, 32–35, 114, 120, 129
Being, 31–35, 63–64, 114, 119–20, 129
Bendis, 72
Benson, H., 139
Bloom, A., 8, 27–28, 65, 98, 115, 118
Bobonich, C., 17–20, 22, 26, 28, 49
Brown, E., 74
Burnyeat, M., 74–76, 91

Calculation (*logistikon*), 12–17, 20–21, 23, 28, 32, 39, 45, 63, 74, 89–90, 95–96, 104, 115–16, 120
Callicles, 40, 143
Cave (allegory of), 31–32, 56, 74–76, 83
Cephalus, 51–55, 70, 73, 88 129
Cherniss, H., 112
Charmides (of Plato), 23–24
City of Pigs, 46, 48, 50, 61, 84, 119
City-soul analogy, 10, 15–17, 21, 23, 30, 49, 110
Clay, D., 69
Cleitophon, 71
Collection, 134, 138
Comedy, 43
Cooper, J., 18, 86, 94

Death, 42, 71, 96, 122
Demagogue, 87, 90
Democracy, 2, 77–88, 90–93, 101, 103, 131, 151
Desire, 12–18, 20–25, 28, 39, 47–49, 52, 63, 67, 74, 84, 88–89, 95–96, 103–4
Dialectic, 3, 5–6, 35, 133–52
Dialegsthai ("to converse"), 7, 54–55, 133, 136, 141–47, 149
Dionysus, 43
Diversity, 2, 72, 83–86, 92, 127–28, 131
Divided Line, 31–32, 34–40, 54–55, 63, 95, 115, 150
Division, 134–38
Dorter, K., 137
Dreams, 81–82, 89–90, 97, 103–4

Education, 31–32, 36–37, 40
Eleatic Stranger, 135–36, 145
Elenchus ("refutation"), 139, 142–43
Epistēmē *("knowledge")*, 37
Er (myth of), 83–85, 121–31
Eros, 4, 44–46, 48–69, 73, 76–77, 81, 92, 100, 109–10, 119–20, 129
Eternity, 27, 29, 33
Euben, P., 79–80, 93
Eugenics, 60–61, 92

Factionalism, 43–45, 60, 73
Family, 45, 50, 57, 59–60
Ferrari, G., 138
Fine, G., 66
Forms, 12, 26, 34–35, 55, 64–66, 68, 90, 104, 107–8, 110–113, 117, 119–29, 134, 139–40, 149–50
Freedom, 81–82, 85–86, 101, 128–29, 131, 151
Freud, S., 49

Gadamer, H., 142–43
Geometry, 40
Gill, C., 141, 144

Glaucon, 3–4, 6–7, 11, 29, 40, 43, 46–47, 49–50, 55–57, 60, 70–71, 75, 83–84, 88, 119
Gomez-Lobo, A., 136
Gonzalez, F., 142
Gordon, J., 141–42
Gorgias (of Plato), 40, 142–43
Griswold, C., 91, 112–14, 130, 134–35, 144, 147
Gyges, 43, 70–71

Hegel, G., 5–6, 147–48
Heraclitus, 26, 113
Hesiod, 41, 52, 70
Homer, 41–43, 111, 115
Homunculus, 16
Hyland, D., 48, 55, 69
Hypothesis, 36, 137–38, 149–50

Idea ("idea"), 10, 12, 110
Idea of the Good, 31, 63, 66–68, 95, 127–28
Images, 31, 34
Imitation, 111–20
Immortality (of the soul), 105–7, 121–22
Irony, 91, 93, 112
Irwin, T., 18
Isocrates, 144

Justice, 7, 11–12, 33, 38, 43, 53, 55, 93

Kahn, C., 17, 48–49, 133, 141, 149
Kallipolis ("beautiful city"), 8–9, 11, 37–48, 52, 55, 57–58, 60–61, 68–78, 81, 83, 85–88, 91–93, 103, 111–13, 128, 131, 150–51
Keuls, E., 59
Klein, J., 12, 21, 33
Kneale, M., and Kneale W., 13, 138–39

Lachesis, 123, 126
Lachterman, D., 67
Laws (of Plato), 106
Lear, J., 20, 30, 96, 102, 107
Leontius, 14, 39, 95–96
Lesses, G., 17
Logos ("rational account"), 6, 8, 29–30, 54–55, 58, 68, 100, 108–9, 111, 121, 130–31, 145
Lyons, J., 133

Many, the, 82, 124–125
Marriage Number, 39, 45, 57, 60–61, 68–69, 88–89

McKim, R., 142
Meno (of Plato), 144, 146
Midas, 99
Money, 97–100, 119
Monoson, S. 80–81, 84, 93
Music, 40–41, 43, 45, 47, 72
Muthos ("myth"), 41, 104, 108–9, 111, 127, 130–31

Narrative, 95, 98, 100, 102, 105–10
Nehamas, A., 32, 53, 112, 114–20
Noble Lie, 44–45, 47, 57
Nussbaum, M., 21

Odysseus, 83, 85, 92, 96, 128–29, 131
Oligarchy, 78, 88, 94, 98–100, 102, 119
Ovid, 99

Parrhēsia ("free speech"), 80–81
Particulars, 108, 130, 134, 144
Parts (of the soul), 26–28, 39, 89–90, 94, 109, 114–16, 118
Penner, T., 20, 102, 104
Phaedo (of Plato), 106, 122
Phaedrus (of Plato), 24, 106, 134–35
Philebus (of Plato), 33, 137
Philosophy, 24–25, 28, 36, 48, 55, 62–64, 67–69, 71, 79–83, 85–86, 89, 119, 124–25, 129, 130, 140. 148–49, 151
Philosopher-Kings, 32, 62, 73
Piraeus, 51, 72, 86
Pleasure, 18
Pleonexia ("having more"), 40
Poetry, 40, 41, 43, 70–71, 111, 113–21, 129–30, 151
Polemarchus, 3, 6, 50–51, 53, 55–57, 72, 88, 129
Principle of Non-Opposition ("PNO"), 6, 13, 21–23, 27, 29–30, 33, 48, 76, 89, 97, 100–101, 108, 110, 115, 117, 120–21, 148
Privacy, 82–83, 128, 131
Protagoras (of Plato), 13, 104, 143, 145–46
Psychē ("soul"), 2

Ricoeur, P., 100
Robinson, R., 28–29, 133, 139–41
Rosen, S., 62, 109, 135, 151
Ryle, G., 139–40

Sachs, D., 7
Samons, L., 80
Saxonhouse, A., 59, 80–81, 83–84, 93

Self-Knowledge, 23–24, 96
Sensation, 32, 34–35
Seventh Letter (of Plato), 127
Smith, N., 31, 35
Sophists, 65
Sophist (of Plato), 135–36, 144
Sophocles, 51–52, 73, 88, 129
Sophrosunē ("moderation"), 25
Soul, 2, 12–16, 20, 22, 29, 89–90, 93, 96, 102–105, 108, 114, 120, 131, 151
Spirit (*thumos*), 12, 14–16, 39, 47, 85, 95–96, 116
Statesman (of Plato), 106, 135–37
Stenzel, J., 136, 141
Stories, 29–30, 94, 97, 105, 108–10, 120, 127, 130–31
Strauss, L., 56, 74–76, 93, 144
Sun, 31–32
Symposium (of Plato), 42, 104–5

Technē, 35–38, 46, 55, 57, 89, 133, 135, 137, 140, 143, 145–46
Theaetetus (of Plato), 53–5, 107, 144–45
Theages, 47, 119

Thrasymachus, 3, 6, 7, 11, 49–50, 56, 71–72
Timaeus (of Plato), 106
Timocracy, 78, 88, 94, 97–98, 100–103
Tripartite Psychology, 2, 6, 12–19, 21–27, 29–30, 38, 48, 49, 63, 68–69, 74, 89, 103, 105–6, 117–19
Tyrant, 52, 55, 57, 73, 78, 81, 86–93, 101, 103, 123–25, 130

Universal, 108, 130, 134

Vlastos, G., 7, 59, 86, 139

War, 47, 85–87, 97
Waves (three), 5, 30, 38, 49–50, 57–69, 88–89, 95
What-is-it Question, 53–55, 68, 107, 130, 144
Whitehead, A., 33–34
Williams, B., 15–22, 26, 28, 49
Wittgenstein, L., 65, 82, 107–8

Zeno, 139